ALABAMA FOLK PLAYS

THE CAROLINA PLAYMAKERS SERIES

Frederick H. Koch, *Editor*

Mexican Folk Plays
by Josephina Niggli

Folk Plays of Eastern Carolina
by Bernice Kelly Harris

Alabama Folk Plays
by Kate Porter Lewis

Canadian Folk Plays
by Gwen Pharis Ringwood
(in preparation)

Smoky Mountain Comedies
by Fred Koch, Jr.
(in preparation)

Wootten-Moulton

THE HOME OF THE CAROLINA PLAYMAKERS, THE FIRST THEATRE BUILDING IN AMERICA TO BE DEDICATED TO THE MAKING OF ITS OWN NATIVE DRAMA.

ALABAMA
FOLK PLAYS

By KATE PORTER LEWIS

EDITED, *with an Introduction by*
FREDERICK H. KOCH
Founder and Director of
THE CAROLINA PLAYMAKERS

*Illustrated with photographs
from the original productions*

Chapel Hill
THE UNIVERSITY OF NORTH CAROLINA PRESS

A royalty fee is required for each performance of any of these plays, either by amateurs or by professionals. Special arrangements must be made for radio broadcasting.

The acting rights to these plays are controlled by Samuel French, 25 West 45th Street, New York, N. Y., or 811 West 7th Street, Los Angeles, Calif., and in Canada by Samuel French (Canada) Limited, 480 University Avenue, Toronto, to whom application should be made for production.

COPYRIGHT, 1943, BY
THE UNIVERSITY OF NORTH CAROLINA PRESS

TO MY FATHER

OSCAR RICHARDSON PORTER

PLAYS OF
THE DEEP SOUTH

In *Alabama Folk Plays* we see the drama of the lives of a humble folk—black and white—living in the back-country of that region familiarly known as "The Deep South."

The author avers that in the memory of old slaves a shower of stars fell on Alabama and cast a spell over all the land. Her plays introduce us to the folk who inhabit this land—this teeming red earth ploughed by surging rivers—a land of brooding silences, of swamps and dark bayous, of deep forests and sunlit grassy hills. It is still a land of enchantment for all the children of Alabama, and it always will be.

Born in Greenville, Alabama, Kate Porter Lewis recalls vividly the rambling old house in which her family had lived for generations and the happy childhood she spent there. More vivid still are memories of her early years spent at her grandfather's sawmill village in the heart of a vast forest of virgin timber.

"For the longest time," she laughs, "I thought virgins were giant pines. It was disillusioning to discover that they might be mere old maids."

From the days when she was a little girl making up plays for the white children of the mill village and the young darkies of the "Quarters," she was impelled to write. "I get more of a thrill out of writing," she said to me one day, "than anything else except having a new baby!"

Mrs. Lewis' interest in playwriting brought her to Chapel Hill. Having finished a new play, she decided late one afternoon that she would like to see it produced at The Playmakers Theatre. By midnight she had a tenant in her Tuscaloosa house; and before daybreak of the following morning she was loading her four children, her Negro Mammy, and the dog, into the family car. The rent check fluttering from one hand, for the ink of the signature was not yet dry, she began the six-hundred-mile drive to Chapel Hill. What was the teaching fellowship she had held, even at her own state university, compared to seeing the characters of her own play come alive on a stage? There had been rôles to play at the Birmingham Little Theatre and parts in amateur plays in various other southern towns. But to see and to hear one's own characters on the stage of The Playmakers Theatre! ...

"I did not know whether I'd be able to find a vacant house in Chapel Hill, or whether I'd be able to pay my college fees beyond that first quarter," she confessed, "but I had made the start I had long wanted to make. And for me, at least, all the road sang all the way."

Immediately upon her arrival in Chapel Hill, Mrs. Lewis enrolled in the playwriting course and began to write all manner of plays of her native state, both of the white folk and of the Negroes—so many in fact that we could not produce all of them. I remember remarking to her, "Alabama is certainly a country of great fertility. Keep it up. We'll produce all of your plays yet!" In 1939 she was awarded the Master of Arts degree in Dramatic Art at the University of North Carolina, submitting in lieu of the traditional thesis a full-length folk play of Alabama, "Jed's Lamp."

The plays in the present volume were produced originally in The Playmakers Theatre at Chapel Hill, where they found an eager audience. In her Negro comedies the author shares with her characters their innate enjoyment of everyday life, their love of the land, of their homes and their children. She treasures their warm friendliness and their natural abandon to the pleasures of the good earth. She has recorded their moments of exuberance and childish delight. She tells the stories of their simple lives in their own pungent vernacular and in the natural rhythms of their songs and their dancing feet. And she holds with them their firm faith in the life to come and interprets for us their glorious expectation of an earthly paradise beyond the grave.

THE SCARLET PETTICOAT

This story comes from the Black Belt where the Negroes considerably outnumber the whites. The young widow, Evalina, cherishes a desire for a life that will insure her everlasting salvation and unite her forever with her dead husband. She finds it hard, however, to endure her lonely widowhood and cannot bring herself to give up entirely her love of gay color and the brightness of the earth. "Mandy's determination to prolong the days of mourning for her son illustrates not so much a morbid wish to dwell on death," the author holds, "as the desire of the lowly Negro to extend the deference accorded a mourner by sympathetic neighbors." Funerals, like baptizings, especially in streams "whar you kin come up straightway out'n de water lak Jesus come out o' Jordan," and weddings with their accompanying feasting and merriment—to say nothing of an impressive "pair o' co't house licenses" and even frequent "bornin's"—lend a sense of importance to the lowly as well as to those in high places.

THREE LINKS O' CHAIN

In *Three Links O' Chain* we have a characteristic figure of our southern scene, the guitar-playing troubadour. Skip is just such a vagabond musician as used to be found in almost every part of the South. He wandered about from place to place "co'tin' some likely gal" or serenading the white folks under the moonlit veranda of the Big House, rendering with equal feeling the gay songs or "sorry" songs that God gives. Sometimes he is the leader of one of the small Negro "orkistris" to the strains of which Alabama folk have danced away many a night in many an ante-bellum town. Such makers of homemade music are still to be found in the "Sad'dy night frolics" and in the "big meetin's" of a Sunday in the Dark Belt towns of the South.

WATERMELON TIME

"Judged by conventional standards," Mrs. Lewis says, "my humble friends of *Watermelon Time* might be considered unmoral. Born alike of a harmony with nature, are their unquenchable delight in earthly pleasures and their irrepressible religious zeal. Matching the rhythm of their mellow spirituals are the unerring patterns of their frenzied dancing feet."

Here then are primitive children of the Southland glorying alike in the satisfaction of their natural physical desires and in their spiritual yearnings for immortality—

blessed irresponsibles they are, whom civilization has left unspoiled and society has not yet "uplifted."

PARTY DRESS

Two plays in this volume, *Party Dress* and *The Ivory Shawl*, present the lonely lives of pitifully poor white women living in the sparsely settled back-country of southern Alabama, far away from the currents of modern life.

The scene of *Party Dress* is the kitchen-living room of the Benson farmhouse, in which pretty young Martie lives with her brother and sister-in-law. Martie is the daughter of a seamstress who designed and made gowns for the town folk but could not afford to make for herself anything but the plain drab work-dress of her daily life. Mrs. Lewis recalls the dim lamplit room of such a seamstress littered with soft silks and lovely cotton prints waiting to be fashioned as garments for more fortunate women. "Once I saw a woman kneeling on a rough floor," she says, "bare except for scattered scraps of gay silks and velvets that shone strangely on the old unpainted boards. The woman knelt to mark the hem of a Mardigras costume while a debutante stood for a fitting. As she measured the spangled hem of the ball dress, a hungry baby worried her withered breast."

The play is the simple story of Martie, who remembers her childhood in such surroundings and who craves a little beauty and joy of a new party dress of her own.

THE IVORY SHAWL

The Ivory Shawl shows the awakening of a woman who thought her soul had died, of Mattie Walker, farm wife and mother, who lives in the back room of a crossroads store in a remote section of southern Alabama. It is the story of a woman who triumphs over her environment and lives again in the future she plans for her daughter, Martha. An old embroidered shawl, packed away long years, symbolizes, for Mattie, the romance of her youth. When Martha unpacks the shawl and stands enveloped in its silken folds, Mattie suddenly recalls the life she has lost. With supreme courage and sacrifice she plans better things for her daughter. *The Ivory Shawl* is in a sense a sequel to *Party Dress*. Mattie (who was Martie in *Party Dress*), haunted the author, she tells me, until she wrote the story of her daughter in *The Ivory Shawl*.

The *Alabama Folk Plays* are favorites in our Playmakers' repertory. They may be produced simply on school and little stages in any section of the country.

FREDERICK H. KOCH

Chapel Hill, North Carolina
July 20, 1942

A FOREWORD
BY THE AUTHOR

SOME SAY that stars fell on Alabama. I've heard it as a child—from silver-haired old ladies, star-dust in their eyes twinkling with laughter. And the Indian Chief in the bayou has made of this legend a song to thunder through cypress and liveoak and pine—the old red Chief who remembers how the stars rained down like hail, blinding him, yet flooding his soul with light.

Once when the lightning flashed on a cloudless day, a fearful whisper swept across a field, and darkies knelt between long white cotton rows .To my childish imagination, the familiar figures became ebony statues set between aisles of snowball bushes planted in reddest earth. A wail shivered the stillness, and my small body seemed to root itself on the edge of the broad field. An hundred suppliant hands were raised to heaven, clenched above arms lifted like pairs of black swords, blade to blade, above the white bolls. My body quivered with something not akin to fear as I heard a chorus chant a rhythmic prayer to:

> That Lily of the Valley,
> That Morning Star . . .

I know not how nor when stars fell on Alabama. But I have long known that a miracle of some kind cast a spell on my land. Guided by the loving hands of Vicky, my little black nurse, I wandered through the dense pine forest surrounding my grandfather's sawmill village. There Vicky discovered a secret she did not tell my older brother or Black Willie, the gardener's boy. Only I was told that the big blue violets peeping through the brown pine straw, and the first spring daisies in the meadow back of "the Big House," were stars that had fallen. Were not these flowers shaped like stars, and were they not the color of heaven itself?

Hurrying home through the dark wood after stolen visits to the fish pond with the alligators and the water-lilies in it, Vicky and I darted through the tall pines with skirts drawn protectingly over our heads. Were not the stars we glimpsed through the black boughs ready to rain down punishment at any moment?

After such escapades it was comforting to lie safe in my crib and look up at stars that smiled down like friendly faces. Sometimes I dared to put my hand out the window by my bed and touch a magnolia bloom that, just before I fell asleep, became for me the calm white evening star God sent down as a sign of His forgiveness.

It was Aunt Ginsie whom I first heard talking to Jesus as though He stood close beside us. Aunt Ginsie had a right to talk to Jesus about 'most anything. She even stood up straight and talked to God any time she took a notion. But that was because she didn't always have time to go to the white, steepled church my grandfather built on the hill for the mill villagers, or even to kneel wherever she was. God, you see, handed all the village children He created in His image, white and black, straight out of His lap into Aunt Ginsie's lap. Aunt Ginsie saw your baby brothers and sisters even before you knew they were coming. As soon as they were born she bathed them and dressed them and praised God that she was His handmaid. When folks died she bathed them and dressed them again and praised God just the same.

The first time I heard Aunt Ginsie talking to Jesus I wondered why she didn't tell Him about our new baby instead of talking to Him about Mama. That night, when my little brother lay dying, Aunt Ginsie waked me in the dark. As she hurriedly buttoned my clothes she told me she had to go deep into the wood before dawn and talk to the Morning Star the Bible told about. When she left, a hush descended on the house and everything grew cold and gray. No one had time for me and I stood alone at the window and waited while Aunt Ginsie prayed. After awhile I knew that I should never be afraid of anything in the heavens again. I was glad God had told Jesus to light up the world like the morning star.

It was my mother who taught me to spell but it was Aunt Ginsie who compelled me to read. While she prepared our meals or while she and Vicky washed and dried the dishes, I sat in my low hickory chair by the kitchen fireplace and read from the heavy family Bible on my knees. In the afternoons Aunt Ginsie sometimes took me to her cabin on the far edge of the pasture. There I was told to read "the Word" to her while she washed and ironed. But in the cabin I lost interest in the Bible and insisted on reading the newspapers pasted on all the walls of the house. By climbing on the furniture I could trace even the topmost lines of print. Yet to this day I wonder what words were hidden in one of those sections of "wall paper." I could not spell out this portion because it was covered by a large picture of a fat black angel with spreading white wings and a voluminous white robe. The angel held a wreath of forget-me-nots in her hand and was flying down to place the garland on the head of Aunt Ginsie's husband, a little ginger-colored man in a lower corner of the mat, cut off just below his drooping shoulders by the wide gilt frame.

Although Aunt Ginsie's husband had died a preacher, he was somehow associated in my mind with disappearing chickens, and I did not think he deserved the crown. But I was relieved to know there were Negro angels in heaven who did not hold everything against people. There was, of course, something incongruous about a heavy black angel who did not in any way resemble a slender boy angel over a baby's grave, or even the grown-up angels on Christmas- and Easter-cards; yet I hoped Aunt Ginsie wouldn't be a white angel in the other world. It comforted me to think she might be in that formal heaven I had heard about at the village Sunday school. I wondered if the white angels would ever let her put down her golden harp and sing the spirituals of her own people instead of chanting the doleful hymns our choir sang.

When I had learned to read the Bible to Aunt Ginsie's satisfaction she began to take Vicky and me to baptizings. She said we had to learn to wash our souls clean as well as our bodies. Though I did not approach the baptismal ceremonies with the reverence due them, I began to look on the creeks about us as hallowed waters. And when I was told that my great-grandmother, a pioneer before Alabama was a state, was the first woman baptized in the Alabama river, that red stream took on a sanctity unrivaled by Jordan in the Holy Land or the Confederate Capitol in Montgomery.

Gradually the land became, not my grandfather's timber land, but God's land. I knew somehow, that had the

Bible never been written, many of His messages might still have been read. His alphabet was everywhere in the forest, in the grasses of the meadow, and in the sky, for those who would translate His words.

Perhaps my first spiritual lesson was voiced in an expression of my childish delight in a thunder storm:

> I saw gold letters flash across
>   A purple sky today—
> And tried to read the words they spelled—
>   But they all skipped away!
>
> I could not see the hand that wrote
>   In brightness like a flame,
> And yet I knew that it was God
>   Who signed His holy name!

One April the pine forest seemed mystic rather than enchanted. Many had come out of the baptismal streams shouting that they had seen Jesus. Vicky was among this number and as Easter drew near it pleased her to fancy that Jesus had again walked on the earth and had caught His trailing robe on the flowering thorn and dogwood trees as He passed through the wood. I did not help my mother weave white branches into wreaths for the altar that Easter. Clustered stars of dogwood bloom and fragrant thorn had become forever symbols of a shining raiment glimpsed by dark eyes drenched with the sacred waters of my land. Long after Vicky's revelation I tried to capture her impression in words:

> White was His raiment that first Easter morn—
> White as the dogwood and budding thorn:
> White is His raiment ... *so white, still,*
> In deep April valley, on high April hill!

The virgin pine forest is gone now; but throughout Alabama, among the young pines, magnolia and dogwood still gleam like new-fallen stars.

K.P.L.

Tuscaloosa, Alabama

CONTENTS

	PAGE
PLAYS OF THE DEEP SOUTH	vii
by Frederick H. Koch	
A FOREWORD	xiii
by the Author	
THE SCARLET PETTICOAT	1
A Comedy of the Black Belt	
THREE LINKS O' CHAIN	33
A Play of Negro Country Folk	
WATERMELON TIME	63
A Comedy of the Black Belt	
PARTY DRESS	93
A Play of the Back Country	
THE IVORY SHAWL	125
A Play of the Back Country

ILLUSTRATIONS

The Playmakers Theatre . . . . . *Frontispiece*	
	FACING PAGE
Scene from "The Scarlet Petticoat"	16
Scene from "Three Links O' Chain"	60
Scene from "Watermelon Time"	90
Scene from "Party Dress"	108

THE SCARLET PETTICOAT

A COMEDY OF THE BLACK BELT

Written in the playwriting course at the University of North Carolina and originally produced by The Carolina Playmakers on May 6, 1940.

THE CHARACTERS

EVALINA, *a young widow* — Frances Goforth
MANDY HAWKINS, *her mother-in-law* — Elizabeth Blair
JANIE DULIN, *a mourner*
　three times in her own right — Marguerite Goodman
JIM POSEY, *a dealer in tombstones* — Richard Porter Lewis

SCENE: The "front room" of a Negro cabin on the outskirts of Marion, Alabama.

TIME: June, 1940. "Up in de mawnin'."

THE SCENE

It is mid-morning of a June day in Marion, Alabama. Through the open doorway of MANDY HAWKINS' *white-washed cabin one glimpses pink myrtles framing a rickety front porch and, beyond a box-bordered walk, bending over a sagging gate weighed down by bloom. Honeysuckle vines interlace the mis-matched palings of an old, unpainted fence as if in one last effort to bind together the patched, decaying wood. Crowding close to the porch on both sides of the steps, the thick, glossy foliage of cape jasmine screens the lace-curtained window on either side of the open door. Both bushes have been stripped of their blossoms, and a single bud, strangely white in* EVALINA'S *mop of kinky hair, is all that remains of the waxen flowers whose fragrance filled cabin and dooryard earlier in the day.*

A sense of order pervades MANDY'S *"front room" with its freshly-laundered curtains of coarse lace, its bare walls and floor scrubbed clean, and its broad chimney of white-washed brick. The fireplace, screened by a home-made frame pasted with gaily-colored advertisements cut from old calendars, projects from the left wall, and a door opening into* MANDY'S *bedroom leads, in turn, to the kitchen. In the upper-left corner of the room is an old chest of drawers with small mirror. On the marble top of the chest are a pair of light-blue china vases and a matching tray. Close to the window at the right of the front door, its back against the right wall, is a sturdy* walnut "four-poster bed." Its fat feather pillows are neatly covered by starched "shams," its high mattress spread with a "Star of Bethlehem" quilt so generous of length and breadth, so resplendent of color, as to call to mind every star of the "firma-mint." Down-right is an organ of the type still used in country churches of the South, and prized also in country homes where hymns are sung on "weeky days" as well as on Sundays. Near the center of the room is a small pine table covered with a hem-stitched white cloth. On the table is a kerosene lamp of glass, with globular cranberry shade. Beside the lamp, is the inevitable library of the southern negro, literate or illiterate, "The Word," in its usual cheap black binding. A low, splint-bottomed rocker stands at the left of the table, and facing it near the foot of the bed, is a matching straight chair. A similar chair is precisely placed before the window at the left of the front door.

EVALINA, seated on a stool before the organ, raises her plump, ginger-colored face toward heaven. The hymnal is open before her but she does not glance at it as she faithfully renders the accompaniment of "Nearer my God to Thee." EVALINA'S young body is enveloped in a plain mourning-dress of black cotton, high-necked, long-sleeved, and covering her ankles. No sound issues from her full red mouth, and her uplifted, child-like face remains rapt as she seems to express all the loneliness of her soul in the plaintive notes of the funeral hymn.

Suddenly an original but none-the-less rhythmic version of the accompaniment peals from the organ. EVALINA'S soft eyes twinkle and unconsciously she tosses her head from side to side. Her vigorously pedaling feet mark time to the jazzed tune while her deft hands pluck at stops and chords as with wild desire to wring from the instru-

ment some repressed exultation. Finally her lithe body, from the soles of her restless feet to the tips of her eager, tingling fingers, weaves and twists through the rhythm of the dancing melody.

Unobserved by EVALINA, *her mother-in-law,* MANDY HAWKINS, *comes up the front walk, and after a startled pause on the porch, steals inside the doorway. A gaunt, black woman wearing a dress of the same material and pattern as* EVALINA'S, MANDY *throws back her mourning-veil draping her cheap straw sailor hat and stares at* EVALINA *who is now writhing with the very joy of living. Her scrawny arms akimbo, her face wrinkling with indignation,* MANDY *restrains the wrath that wells to her lips until her mouth and jaws work convulsively and her withered cheeks swell as if threatened by angry words seeking escape.*

But EVALINA *seems to sense the glaring eyes. And as if subdued by the hostile presence of* MANDY, *the organ notes grow slower and fainter. Glancing toward her right,* EVALINA *records her impression by a look of terror accompanied by a crashing discord. Gradually recovering her poise, she launches into a repetition of her first pious rendition of the hymn, her posture finally assuming a dignity calculated to render any widow beyond reproach.*

MANDY (*coming down toward* EVALINA). I heerd you de fus' time! I heerd you and I seed you! (*Muttering.*) Jazzin' up dat church-hymn. (*Pausing near the organ as* EVALINA, *who has abruptly brought the hymn to a close at the sound of* MANDY'S *voice, reluctantly turns on the stool to face her accuser.*) How-come you got to go devilin' de very chune de mo'ners sung over Henry's grave?

EVALINA. But Ma Hawkins, ever'body laks joyful chunes sometime. Seem lak folks gits tired o' mo'nful songs.

MANDY. Seems lak some folks gits tired o' mo'nin' fer dey daid husband mighty quick. Dat's how it seem! *(Standing directly in front of* EVALINA.*)* Fum now on, hit'll be you what totes de washin' to and fum Miss Ellen's house. I ain't leavin' nobody to mess wid my orgin. *(Muttering to herself as she turns away.)* Six mont' a widder, and cuttin' up lak dat!

EVALINA. Aw now, Ma Hawkins, Henry laked jazz chunes. He say so he own self. *(Studying first one dull leather shoe and then the other, she twists her ankles in their coarse black stockings.)* Course he wa'n't so good at keepin' time wid 'em. Not dancin' to 'em, he wa'n't. *(Naïvely, as she looks up.)* But den, Henry wa'n't none too peart no time.

MANDY. My boy wa'n't sot on foolishness! *(Shaking a bony finger at* EVALINA.*)* And you better git yo' heart sot on salvation 'fo' you lays yo'self down wid Henry in dat graveyard out yonder. *(Pointing toward the sloping hillside beyond her dooryard.)*

EVALINA *(slowly rising to stare beyond the doorway).* Hit sho' would be a long time to sleep out dere by yo' lone self, all right. *(Suddenly she turns toward* MANDY *who removes her hat and veil and lays them on the table.)* I'se got a heap o' nights to lay in my own bed, here *(pointing toward the "four-poster")* 'fo' I starts sleepin' in de graveyard.

MANDY *(sinking wearily into the rocker).* Yeh, Evalina, you is young, and you is got to lay alone fer a spell.

(*Beginning to rock slightly as* EVALINA *takes a step toward the bed and stands looking down at the bright quilt.*) But yo' time'll come. (MANDY *slips off a shoe, takes from it a fifty-cent piece, and holds it up for* EVALINA *to see.*) Fo' bits! (*Proudly.*) Miss Ellen gimme extry fer de men's white pants.

EVALINA (*coming slowly over to the table*). Miss Ellen say she gwine send all her curtains to you since I done washed her winders.

MANDY. Dem curtains'll need washin' if she send 'em by dat Janie Dulin she done hired fer a nuss-maid.

EVALINA (*playing with the lamp-shade*). Miss Janie sho' laks nussin' jobs. (*Wistfully, as she leans against the table, her back to* MANDY.) Pushin' baby-cyarts 'roun' de town and settin' on street co'ners *is* sort o' friendly-like. (*Regretfully.*) I wisht I'd a-knowed Miss Ellen wanted a nuss-maid.

MANDY (*sharply*). Baby-tendin' ain't no fittin' job fer gals widout husbands! (*Practically.*) Wid Miss Ellen payin' me extry fer big washin's, us kin git up de money fer dat double tombstone, anyways.

EVALINA (*a bit sorrowfully as she lets her hands fall to her sides and shakes her head while looking at her bed*). Henry sho' had his heart sot on dat double monu*mint*.

MANDY (*picking up her fan, and waving it back and forth in rhythmic movements until she begins to emphasize her words with both fan and rocker*). Well,

didn't you and Henry always lay yo' heads side by side on dem goose-fedder pillows? Hit'll seem natural, chile, you and Henry restin' together wid two marble slabs spread over you clost as dey kin git. (*Shaking her head with satisfaction.*) Lak a solid white counterpane kiverin' you bofe. And one big headstone, lak de headpiece o' yo' bed, dere. (*She examines the coin in the palm of her hand, squinting at it as she slowly turns it in a circular motion, and finally slips it into a pocket of her dress as she looks up at* EVALINA.)
Tain't gwine be long now 'fo' us kin tell dat Jim Posey to set up dat tombstone he been a-cuttin' out dat big hunk o' marble. Soon us kin quit strippin' dem cape jesmine bushes ever' day and kiver up dat mound o' red dirt wid a pyore white slab.

EVALINA (*sighing as she sits down opposite* MANDY). Dat sho' will be nice, Ma Hawkins. (*Wilting.*) De hot sun wilts down dem po' jesmines 'most quick as I kin pull 'em off de bushes and tote 'em to de graveyard.

MANDY (*looking at* EVALINA *suspiciously*). Seems lak dey's one jesmine what ain't wiltin' in no sun! (EVALINA *guiltily touches her hair.*) Tain't becomin' to no mo'ner to primp herself up dat-a-way.

EVALINA. But Henry useter lak me all fixed up, Ma Hawkins.

MANDY (*abruptly, as* EVALINA *rises and preens herself*). Henry wa'n't daid, den. (*Vehemently, as she leans forward in her chair.*) And what you think dat sassy Jim Posey gwine say ifn he come by to git a pay*mint* on yo' husband's tombstone and find you diked out lak dat?

EVALINA *(innocently)*. Jim Posey ain't gwine kere. *(Sitting on the side of the bed and twining her arm about the bed-post at foot.)* Him and Henry bofe useter bring me *bow*-kays when dey come courtin'. *(Reminiscently as she spreads her arms at her sides resting her palms on the quilt as she leans back.)* Jim Posey, he say dat last time, when he brung dat big bunch o' lilacs, I was lak a flower my own self, ripe fer de bloomin'.

MANDY. Humph! A heap o' good it done 'im to keep his ma's flower-beds stripped.

EVALINA *(simply)*. Dat's what Henry tole 'im.

MANDY *(smiling over her memories)*. Henry sho' laked de smell o' dem cape jesmines. *(With sudden energy.)* But me and you is got to git a move on us ifn we gits dat slab layed down 'fo' dem jesmines stops bloomin'. *(As EVALINA rises.)* How much you done put in dat bakin'-powder can by dis time?

EVALINA *(hesitantly, as she walks toward the organ in an effort to appear casual)*. I *had* three dollars dis mawnin'.

MANDY. Humph! Same as you had last week. *(Gently as she concentrates on drawing on her shoe.)* But den, lak I been a-tellin' Jim Posey, a widder is got to take time to mo'n. *(Rising slowly.)* Us bofe better be addin' what we kin to de fund do'. Looks lak us got to fill dat bakin'-powder can and dat coffee-can, too, if us honors Henry proper.

EVALINA (*as* MANDY *starts toward the doorway at left*). Hit sho' gwine take a heap o' dimes to fill dat bakin'-powder can, Ma Hawkins.

MANDY (*turning to face* EVALINA). Don't you fret 'bout de hard work, chile. God-willin', tain't gwine be long 'fo' us bofe lays down to sleep—me and you 'longside o' Henry—and Henry's pappy t'other side o' me.

EVALINA (*twining her arm about the bed-post and gazing down at the starred quilt*). Seems lak I done fell out wid sleep of late.
(JANIE DULIN, *a stout, yellow negress in a starched cotton print that seems more vivid because of a white cap and apron, suddenly flounces into the room. On her head she carries an enormous bundle wrapped in wrinkled brown paper. But this burden, like the heavier ones she has borne, is no hindrance to* JANIE *with the irrepressible laugh and the saucy air that belie her forty years. Or is it fifty years* JANIE *has been prancin' among us in such gay finery as she could piece together?*)

JANIE (*taking in the downcast* EVALINA *at a glance*). And tain't no wonder you don't hanker atter rest! Jes' look at dat! Mopin' 'roun' de bed-post lak you done lost yo' last hope! (*Gazing down at the bed.*) Well, dat Star o' Bethlehem quilt sho' don't become you now.

MANDY (*severely*). If Evalina's got air hope, Janie Dulin, hit's hope o' livin' righteous so she kin jine Henry in de next world! Evalina's a self-respectin' widder 'oman, same as I is.

JANIE (*unabashed, as she comes farther down and pauses to look* MANDY *and* EVALINA *up and down*). Hit's clear to see Henry's bein' respected. (*Glancing from one mourner to the other and shaking her head hopelessly.*) I 'clare 'fo' goodness, Miss Hawkins, dis' place puts me in mind o' a buzzart roost. (*She places the curtains on the table.*)

MANDY (*indignantly, her arms folded*). Look here, gal, is you fergittin' hit's de deceased-ed's Ma you is talkin' to?

JANIE (*calmly*). Naw, Miss Hawkins, I sees you. But hit's de fus' time I'se seed you, and Evalina, too, since Henry's funeral, come last New Year! 'Course you bofe been dere in de amen corner ever' Sunday, all right. But, lak I tole Miss Ellen when she sont me down here wid dese curtains, (*Indicating the curtains by a sharp slap on the brown paper.*) you mo'ners is wropped up in black crepe same as a cocoon winds he-self up! (*Standing back of the table and looking from* MANDY *to* EVALINA.) "I'll be glad to tote dis passel o' washin' down to de Hawkinses," I says to Miss Ellen. "I wants to see if dem mo'ners is as sorry a sight *under* all dat crepe as dey is on the *out*side."

MANDY. Us look mo'nful, and us is mo'nful. And what's mo', us gwine stay mo'nful. And dat's more'n I kin say fer you, Janie Dulin, air time you laid air one o' yo' husbands away!

EVALINA *(placatingly)*. You hadn't oughter vex Ma Hawkins, Miss Janie, and she a mo'ner. *(Hopelessly as she glances down at her dress.)* I reckon us do look mighty doleful. *(With more spirit, as the light of reason inspires her.)* But ifn hit's a buzzart roost dis house puts you in mind of, you oughter 'member Henry's sho' nuff daid.

MANDY *(firmly)*. And if you come here wid any notion' o' gittin' Evalina to gallivant 'roun' wid you, she ain't studyin' no sech! Evalina got her mind sot on salvation. *(Picking up her hat from the table and putting it on.)* But bein' as you is got a mouf big enough fer you and me too, I'll be gittin' on to my washtubs.

JANIE *(overcome by curiosity)*. Law, Miss Hawkins, you don't wash clothes wid a hat and veil on, does you?

MANDY. Us ain't no hypocrites. Us honors de daid in our own yards, front and back, same as when us leaves dis place.
(MANDY deftly tucks her skirts under her belt until they almost reach her knees. Dropping her veil, she picks up the curtains and starts toward the doorway at the left. Suddenly she turns, walks over to EVALINA, and snatches the flower from her hair. EVALINA and JANIE stare after her as she leaves the room, the jasmine crumpled in her hand.)

EVALINA *(disconsolately)*. Ma Hawkins sho' sets a pow'- ful store by mo'nin' clothes. *(Shyly reproachful, she turns to* JANIE.) You wa'n't thinkin' I aimed to fergit Henry a'ready, was you, Miss Janie?

JANIE (*seating herself in the rocker*). Aw, fer land's sakes, Evalina, let Henry rest in peace. I ain't come here to stir up nobody. Do' hit do seem to me, Miss Hawkins enjoys her bereave*mint* same as some folks enjoys po' health. And to speak puffickly true, Evalina, you and her bofe is done over-stretched yo' grievin' time.

EVALINA (*leaning toward* JANIE, *her hands on the table*). Now look a-here, Miss Janie, ifn you thinks me and Ma Hawkins is gwinter quit respectin' de daid——

JANIE (*abruptly*). I ain't meddlin' wid Miss Hawkins. Ever'body know she old enough to have one foot in de grave. She were old when she come widdered. But when a wife as young as you is done grieved proper, tain't no use to keep on wailin' till you wakes a man out'n his grave!

EVALINA (*starting to cry*). But us is fresh mo'ners, Miss Janie!

JANIE (*as* EVALINA *turns away from her where she stands near the table*). You looks fresh, all right. De way dem tears is a-pourin' out, you puts me in mind o' a jersey cow freshenin' wid a calf.

EVALINA (*sniffling*). You'd cry, too, Miss Janie, if you was lonesome as I is.

JANIE (*sitting back in her chair*). Mebbe so, mebbe so. (*Leaning forward.*) But if I was dat lonesome, dat ain't all I'd do! (*Softening, she flings out a generous palm in a gesture of understanding.*) Look here, chile, ain't I done holp you mo'n fer Henry?

EVALINA (*turning toward* JANIE *who picks up* MANDY's *crepe-bound fan from the table*). I ain't fergittin' yo' sympathy, Miss Janie. (*Looking up.*) And I ain't fergittin' how good you was to Henry when he was ailin'.

JANIE (*with self-satisfaction as she gently fans herself*). But what you is fergittin' is dat I been a widder three times in my own right!

EVALINA (*tearfully, as she sits on the corner of the table*). But you is 'most allus found somebody to console you, Miss Janie.

JANIE. And I reckon you think I done it by hidin' fum mens under a bolt o' black crepe!

EVALINA. Tain't no use fer me to take off dese black gyarmints, Miss Janie. (*Lifting her skirts to dry her eyes, her back toward* JANIE.) I ain't got no thought fer nobody but Henry, nohow. Me and Ma Hawkins (*sobbing.*) . . . we is . . . gwinter always . . . honor Henry . . . wid mo'nin' clo-o-thes. . . .
(*In lifting her skirt,* EVALINA *discloses a bright-red satin petticoat under her mourning dress.* JANIE *leans forward as she stares at the scarlet ruffles. She moves her rocker closer as* EVALINA, *forgetful in her grief, lifts her skirt higher to dry her eyes a second time.* JANIE *cocks her head to the left as she seems to peer as far*

under EVALINA's *dress as her sitting position will permit.* EVALINA *becomes conscious of* JANIE's *curiosity and quickly lowers her black skirt.* JANIE *leans back in her rocker in frank contemplation. There is an embarrassed pause for* EVALINA. *Glancing down to avoid* JANIE's *eyes, she discovers that a scarlet hem is still uncovered. After jerking down her dress she begins to smooth its black folds.*)

EVALINA *(guiltily)*. I reckon hit don't match up so good.

JANIE. I allus knowed black cloth was hard to match but I ain't never heerd o' nobody tryin' to match up black wid red! *(She sits back and chuckles.)* I'se seed widders come out o' mo'nin' a heap o' ways, and I ain't sayin' I allus do it de same way, myself. But you is de fus' 'oman I ever seed come out wrong-side-out! *(She leans forward, an amused smile overspreading her face.)* How long is you been flauntin' dat red satin petticoat, Evalina?

EVALINA *(more at ease as she steps back from the table)*. I ain't zackly flauntin' it, Miss Janie. I ain't aimin' to wear it out de house, none. But wid so much black stuff wropped 'roun' me and Ma Hawkins, I jes' nach'ly hankered atter a speck o' color.

JANIE. You is got what you hankered atter, all right. But hit's a good sign! *(Laughing to herself.)* Jes' show dat petticoat to Jim Posey when he comes to collect fer dat big double tombstone you done ordered, and he'll fergit all about graveyards.

EVALINA *(nervously)*. Jim ain't studyin' 'bout collectin' dis soon, is he, Miss Janie?

JANIE. How I know what Jim Posey studyin' 'bout? *(Rising.)* Fer all I knows, he mought be studyin' 'bout you, same as he useter.

EVALINA *(nervously pulling down her skirt, as* JANIE *crosses back of the table and stands by the bed).* You don't think I gwine flaunt dis petticoat befo' no mens, does you, Miss Janie? I reckon I better take hit off. *(Frightened.)* I wa'n't aimin' fer Ma Hawkins to see it, nuther. *(Clutching* JANIE's *arm.)* You ain't gwine tell nobody, is you, Miss Janie?

JANIE *(calmly)*. Course I ain't, chile—last o' all, Miss Hawkins.

EVALINA *(relieved, as she releases* JANIE's *arm).* Dat's good. *(Cheerfully as she goes toward the chest of drawers.)* Mr. Nate Sims, he say he ain't gwine tell, nuther. *(As she pulls out a drawer and rummages among her clothing.)* I paid 'im cash to make sho', do'. Three dollars I handed 'im crost dat counter. *(Pulling out another drawer and searching its contents, she throws them on the floor.)* But twa'n't nobody but me and Mr. Nate in de commissary when us counted all dem silver dimes. *(There is the sound of creaking wagon wheels at the front gate. A man's strong, husky voice calls "Whoa!"* EVALINA, *failing to notice the sound, turns from the open drawer and the pile of clothing at her feet.)* Law, Miss Janie, I cayn't find my black petticoat! *(Taking a step toward* JANIE *who*

WOOTTEN-MOULTON

THE SCARLET PETTICOAT

EVALINA (*revealing a scarlet petticoat beneath her mourning dress*). Wid so much black stuff wropped 'roun' me and Ma Hawkins, I jes' nach'ly hankered atter a speck o' color.

THE SCARLET PETTICOAT 17

is staring in the direction of the gate from where she stands near the foot of the bed.) I bet I done lef' it in de gyarden-house where I changed to dis red 'un. *(Turning toward the doorway at left.)* I got to go see.

JANIE. Hit's too late to git to no gyarden-house now! Dat's Jim Posey a-climbin' out dat waggin'.

EVALINA *(wheeling from the doorway)*. But Jim ain't said nothin' 'bout collectin' fer de tombstone dis early, Miss Janie. *(Tugging at her belt.)* Oh Lawdy, Miss Janie, what I gwine do? *(Hurriedly crossing in front of the table.)* He'p me slide dis petticoat out fum under dis here shirtwaist. I'se a widder 'oman, Miss Janie! *(Still tugging at her waist as she goes up to* JANIE *who has moved down in front of the organ without apparent concern.)* You is got to he'p me hide dis thing fum Ma Hawkins! *(*JANIE *examines the material of* EVALINA'S *top skirt and steps back doubtfully, letting a fold of the black goods slide through her fingers.)*

JANIE. You come 'fo' Jim Posey widout no petticoat a-tall in dat sleazy black stuff and he'll see slap thoo you.

EVALINA *(beseechingly)*. But Miss Janie, I—

JANIE *(decisively)*. Men is got sharp eyes fer women, Evalina—'specially fer widders!
· *(There is a step on the porch.* JANIE *waits for* EVALINA *to admit the caller but* EVALINA *shrinks back timidly, shaking her head as she smooths her black skirt.* JANIE, *unconsciously preening herself as she puts on*

her *"receiving manner" acquired through the gracious acceptance of much courting, rises to the occasion.)*

JANIE (*pleasantly*). Come on in, man. Don't stand out dere lak you was a-doubtin' yo' welcome.
(JIM POSEY, *a tall, loose-limbed darkie, his angular frame somehow unhampered by an ill-fitting checkered suit, bows himself into the room. Though his large hands have a way of moving in frequent circular motions, they seem to move rhythmically. There is a careless grace about the man, and his mellow voice and broad grin are reassuring. His soft eyes have a surprising way of lighting up his dusky face.*)

JIM (*warmly*). Howdy, Miss Janie. I wa'n't expectin' to find you here. (*Wringing her hand.*) Glad to see you! (*Quickly assuming a funeral air.*) Mawnin', Evalina.

EVALINA (*with conscious dignity*). Mawnin', Mr. Posey.

JANIE. Lawd, Jim, if you ain't been a-cuttin' and a-sellin' tombstones so long, you kin put on de very airs of a corpse. But I knows you. (*Popping her fingers and then dancing gaily about the room, her bright skirt flaring as she circles in front of the table.*) I seen dem capers you was a-cuttin' at de ice-cream supper.

JIM (*his face one big smile as* JANIE *comes to a stand-still near the front door*). I'se a officer in de lodge, Miss Janie. De members 'spects me to cut sumpum 'sides tombstones when de lodge give a *ice*-cream supper. (*Seriously to* EVALINA.) Not meanin' no disrespec' to mo'ners.

EVALINA (*simply*). Tain't nothin' wrong wid bringin' up de doin's o' de lodge, I reckon, Mr. Posey. Henry b'longed he own self.
(JANIE *draws up the chair near the chest and places it at right of table. As she seats herself in the rocker she motions to the chair she has drawn up for* JIM.)

JANIE (*curtly*). Set down, Jim. Evalina ain't had a man aroun' fer so long, she done fergot how to make one feel at home.

EVALINA (*apologetically*). 'Scuse my manners, Mr. Posey. Do take a cheer.

JIM (*awkwardly, as* EVALINA *sits facing him on the organ stool*). Don't kere if I do. (*His feet sprawling before him as he leans back in the chair.*) You're mighty right, Henry b'longed to de lodge, Evalina. And I'se recordin' dat fact right on his tombstone—on his half of it, I means. (*Leaning forward as he plays with his hands.*) Course now, you bein' a woman ... it ain't to say, you understands, womens ain't *fittin'* to jine.... (*Looking apologetically from* EVALINA *to* JANIE.) Naw, sir! Tain't nothin' lak dat! And tain't as if de lodge don't want 'em. But you see, on account o' de ... de custom ... (*Realizing that he is about to involve his reasoning power and hastily summing up the matter.*) Well, womens jes' don't jine, dat's all.

JANIE (*pleasantly*). Well, so long as you-all pays de dues and us women gits invited to de *ice*-cream suppers, I reckon us ain't gwine quarrel 'bout no memberships.

JIM (*snickering*). Law, Miss Janie, ice-cream ain't all you got out de lodge. (*Solemnly, as he turns to* EVALINA.) Lak I tried to tell Henry 'bout inshawnce—Miss Janie, here, is done collected inshawnce offen three lodge members. (*Turning to* JANIE *who is beaming with pride*.) Ain't dat right, Miss Janie?

JANIE. Hit sho' is, Jim. But I done right by ever' one o' dem lodge members same as dey done by me.

EVALINA. You sho' put 'em away nice, Miss Janie. Cayn't nobody say you never done dat.

JIM (*loyally*). Folks come at me talkin' 'bout Miss Janie actin' happy I tells 'em she got a right to frolic wid whosomever and jes' howsomever she please. She done took kere o' three mens in sickness and in health lak she promise. And what's mo', I up and tells 'em, she done laid ever' one o' dem mens out proper.

EVALINA (*impressed*). Got Bible verses writ on all dem slabs, too.

JIM (*assuming the air of a business-man as he rises*). Course now, dat marble slab's a bit thin on dat last grave. But I never said nothin' at de time I put it down. (*Studying the effect of his words on* JANIE.) I figgered when you got dat last install*mint* o' inshawnce, Miss Janie, you'd want to put in a order fer a double monu*mint* lak Henry's. (*After a brief silence*.) I reckon you is figgerin' on bein' put by dat last husband, ain't you, Miss Janie?

JANIE (*indignantly, as she wheels around in her chair*). Who is you, Jim Posey, wid marble dust on yo' clothes —wid de smell o' tombstones on you—to come talkin' to me 'bout my last husband!

JIM. I ain't meanin' you is old, yit, Miss Janie. I'se jes' trying to he'p you look to de future—to save on de cost o' yo' own monu*mint* while you is got de money in hand.

JANIE (*folding her arms*). I wouldn't buy no double monu*mint* ifn you'd put de lodge emblem over me same as my three husbands! I ain't dat anxious to jine up wid nothin'!

JIM (*undefeated, as he leans toward* JANIE). I hope I ain't named de wrong man, Miss Janie. Maybe us could switch one o' dem fus' two heavy slabs over on top o' dat last grave, and—

JANIE. And why-for you reckon I gwine do dat?

JIM (*coming down in front of the table*). Well, den us could put up a double monu*mint* over dat fus' grave and you could lay side o' dat fus' husband—or twixt de fus' *two*, if you ruther.

JANIE (*rising*). I ain't dat anxious to lay dat long wid no man. And not wid no three mens, nuther!

EVALINA (*becoming concerned*). Law, Miss Janie, where is you gwine lay? How you gwine choose twixt all dem mens?

JANIE (*philosophically, crossing to* EVALINA). When a 'oman lays down fer dat long, Evalina, she better lay by her own self. I ain't choosin' *nobody* fer my last rest! And if air one o' dem mens wants to see me when Gabri'l rousts out ever'body, hit's up to dem to look me up!

JIM (*seating himself on the table*). Look a-here, Miss Janie, you ain't studyin' 'bout marryin' agin, is you?

JANIE. Me marry dis soon? (*chuckling, she dances about* JIM). Boy, I ain't had time to enjoy my widderhood, yit. (*Suddenly dropping her arms to her sides.*) Law, lemme git on 'way fum dis place. Miss Ellen gwine have a fit if dat baby wake up and I ain't dere. (*She prances toward the door and then turns to* EVALINA *who stands awkwardly by the organ.*) Don't let 'im hand you out too much sorry talk, gal. He know a better line dan what he been a-givin' out dis mawnin'.

JIM (*slightly embarrassed, looking quickly at* EVALINA *and back at* JANIE). Aw now, Miss Janie, you go 'long.

EVALINA (*rising and following* JANIE *to the door*). As you goes down de road, Miss Janie, would you please to call to Ma Hawkins dat Mr. Posey are come?

JANIE. I'd be proud to do dat, Evalina. (*As she passes through the doorway.*) If dat ain't ol' Peg-leg Johnson! (*Calling as she hurries across the porch, her gay figure distinct as she passes the open window at left.*) Peg! Aw, Peg! (*Her voice still clear, though receding, as she crosses the yard.*) How 'bout you and me steppin' out to de fish-fry, tonight?

JIM (*laughing*). Miss Janie sho' got a knack fer gittin' 'roun'.

EVALINA (*sitting down on the bed*). Miss Janie don't mean no harm. She jes'—jes' useter mens, I reckon.

JIM. She sho' oughter be. But, take old Peg Johnson, out dere (*nodding toward the front door*).—Why, I'd as soon think o' Miss Hawkins or—you—steppin' out to de fish-fry.

EVALINA (*quickly, as she rises*). Me and Ma Hawkins ain't goin' to no frolics. Ain't been to none, nuther!

JIM. Humph. Anybody'd guess dat, all right.

EVALINA (*with innocent frankness, sauntering toward the organ*). Course we likes fish. And *ice*-cream, too.

JIM. Humph! I 'members dat, all right. (*Happily reminiscent as he rises from the edge of the table and leans on the back of the chair to gaze at* EVALINA *who has seated herself on the organ stool.*) How many ice-cream suppers and fish-frys you reckon I done took you to, Evalina?

EVALINA (*primly, as she turns slightly away from him on the stool*). I disremembers, Mr. Posey. (*Folding her hands on her lap.*) My mind is sot on salvation.

JIM (*drily*). So dey tells me.

EVALINA. Ma Hawkins is done got it.

JIM. She got a full dose o' *sumpum*. (*He sits.*) Course now (*placatingly*) lak I was a-tellin' Miss Hawkins down to de marble yard, salvation's a mighty good thing. (*Leaning forward, after a slight pause.*) But look-a here, Evalina, ain't you a mite young to git yo' mind plum sot on hit?

EVALINA (*determinedly, as she looks away from* JIM). My eyes is fixed on hit. (*Uneasily, stealing a glance at him and quickly avoiding his admiring eyes.*) You ain't aimin' to turn me 'roun', is you, Mr. Jim?

JIM (*ignoring her question*). MISTER Jim. Where you git dat?

EVALINA. You fergits, Mr. Jim, I'se a mo'ner.

JIM. Ye-ah. But dat ain't no reason why you got to fergit ol' friends, is it? MISTER Jim. MISTER POSEY. And what's mo', you been treatin' me lak a stranger since you fus' married Henry.

EVALINA (*rising*). My mind is still sot on Henry. (*Her eyes continuing to stare straight before her as she faces front.*) Daid same as livin'.

JIM. Jes' lak Miss Hawkins and her ol' man, hunh?

EVALINA. Dat's de way Henry want it.

JIM (*his ardor thoroughly cooled*). Well, since I come on business, let's us git down to de business. (*Reaching in a pocket of his coat, he draws out a smooth piece of marble, its surface about the size of a sheet of notepaper.*) Course now (*Studying the marble as he rises.*), dis here ain't gwine give you much of a idea, but hit's a sample.

EVALINA. Sample o' which?

JIM (*a trifle impatient*). O' de slab, Evalina. You see, I'se ready to cut yo' name in de head-piece, 'longside o' Henry's name, and I wants to make sho' ever'thing's to yo' likin' 'fo' I spiles de marble.
(EVALINA *takes the sample he has been holding out to her, almost drops it, and quickly hands it back to him.*)

EVALINA (*distastefully*). Hit's too thick.

JIM. Too thick! What kind o' slab does you want? A kiver what'll crack and let de rain run down in yo' coffin?

EVALINA (*panicky as she walks away from him, hurriedly crossing in front of the table*). You hush talkin' to me 'bout coffins, Jim Posey!

JIM. How-come you mind dat? Folks what goes 'roun' shroudin' dey selves in black crepe—

EVALINA (*a bit hysterical, plucking at the collar of her dress as she stands near the door at left*). Dis ain't no shroud!

JIM. Course tain't zackly no shroud, Evalina.

EVALINA (*facing him*). Den how-come you tryin' to bury me?

JIM (*composed*). I ain't trying to bury you, Evalina. You knows I ain't no undertaker.

EVALINA (*muttering to herself, her lips bulging in an angry pout as she turns from him and stares straight ahead*). Mmn-mmn, come at me talkin' 'bout no coffin!

JIM. Look a-here, Evalina, hit's you what's got yo' mind sot on jinin' Henry. If it had-a been lef' up to ME, you wouldn't a-jined up wid 'im livin', let alone daid! (EVALINA, *basking in the warmth of comfort, smiles a little as she slighty raises her black skirt. Before* JIM *sees the scarlet ruffle, however, she jerks down her dress and turns from his ardent gaze.*)

EVALINA (*plainly mustering all the strength of her will*). Look a-here, Jim Posey, don't you be tryin' to turn me 'roun'! (*Still looking resolutely away from him.*) I done tole you—

JIM (*impatiently*). Yeh, I know. You done tole me yo' mind is sot on *Henry*. (*He looks at her critically.*) Well, not meanin' no disrespec', but hit's lak de boys say at de lodge: 'tain't nobody but a daid man gwine wanter tangle he-self up in dat much mo'nin'.
(EVALINA, *recovering from the shock of this final appraisal, studies* JIM *as he looks down at the marble. Still watching him as he turns the sample over in his hands, she moves in front of the table, deliberately raising her skirt. After a brief pause, as he fails to look*

at her, she lifts her skirt higher and arranges the scarlet ruffling to more advantage. JIM *lays the marble on the table. Seeing the mass of scarlet ruffling, he looks searchingly at* EVALINA. EVALINA, *motionless, stares back innocently.*)

JIM (*gazing at the petticoat and then passing the back of his hand over his eyes*). I wonder does you see what I sees? (*Looking inquiringly into* EVALINA'S *expressionless face.*) Is dat bright red thing part o' yo' own clothes, Evalina?

EVALINA (*a little embarrassed, but with a pleased smile, modestly lowering her dress and shyly lifting her eyes to* JIM'S). I reckon some mens does lak color.

JIM (*happy laughter in his voice as he sits down on the organ stool*). Pshaw! Now who'd a-thought— Law, wid dem two kind o' skirts on, look lak me and Henry bofe is in de race, same as befo'!
(*Now* MANDY, *her veil thrown back, her sleeves and skirts tucked up, comes in from the side door. Seeing* JIM, *she pauses just inside the doorway.* JIM, *following the direction of* EVALINA'S *frightened eyes, turns on the stool to meet* MANDY'S *disapproving stare.*)

JIM (*jumping up in an embarrassed manner*). Howdy, Miss Hawkins. I been a-wonderin' why you didn't come in.

EVALINA (*uneasily*). Didn't Miss Janie tell you Mr. Posey was here, Ma Hawkins?

MANDY (*going toward the chest after having lowered her skirts and pulled down her long sleeves*). Dat Janie Dulin ain't tole me nothin'! (*Picking up* EVALINA's *clothing from the floor and placing it in one of the drawers.*) Not since I lef' out dis room, she ain't! I reckon she done found out she done said a-plenty to me.

JIM (*as* MANDY *removes her hat and places it on the chest after having closed the drawer*). I bet she have. More'n a-plenty!

MANDY (*pointedly, coming down to the table*). Hit seem lak a heap o' folks ain't at no loss fer words! (*Contemptuously.*) And now I'll be gittin' you part o' dat pay*mint* you come atter.

JIM. Tain't no hurry, Miss Hawkins.

EVALINA (*nervously backing away*). Naw, Ma Hawkins, Mr. Posey, he say dey ain't no hurry *a-tall*.

MANDY (*to the point*). Den whut he come hyar fer?

JIM. Well, you see, Miss Hawkins, I jes' aimed to see if Evalina—if Widder Hawkins, here (*With a gesture toward* EVALINA.) laked dis sample o' marble I brung along.

MANDY (*examining the marble he hands to her*). Ain't dis de marble you done showed me? (*Laying the sample on the table.*) Ain't it de best you got?

JIM. Yes'm, dat's right, dat's right. Hit sho' is purty marble, all right. (*Crawling out of the difficulty.*) But knowin' de monu*mint's* fer Evalina, too, I thought she mought wanter— (*Breaking off suddenly as he meets* EVALINA's *sullen gaze.*) But hit's fine marble. Dey ain't no two ways 'bout *dat.*

MANDY (*curtly*). Den I'll fetch yo' money. (*She stalks out of the door, left.*)

EVALINA (*hurt and angry*). Now look a-here, Jim Posey! If you thinks I gwine pay you to kiver me over wid dat stuff— (*Pointing to the piece of marble and then dropping her hand hopelessly as her anger melts to tears.*) I reckon you think I got one foot in de grave lak Miss Janie say Ma Hawkins— (*Turning from him as her voice breaks in a sob.*)

JIM (*helpless before her tears*). Aw now, Evalina, I ain't said nothin' lak dat. (*Spreading both palms before her in a gesture of supplication.*) *You* know dat. Why, you—
(MANDY *bursts into the room, a baking-powder can and a coffee-can in her hands. She planks the empty baking-powder can on the table and confronts* EVALINA *with a look of suspicion.*)

MANDY (*to* JIM *as she hands him the coffee-can*). Dere's fo' dollars and six bits. Count it out and put it in yo' pocket whar hit'll be safe. (*Glancing maliciously at* EVALINA.) You kin look to Evalina fer de rest o' dis install*mint.*

EVALINA. But Ma Hawkins, I ain't got—

MANDY (*firmly, as she folds her arms*). You go find dat money, Evalina.

JIM (*putting the money in his pocket after having set the can on the organ*). Dat's all right 'bout de money, Miss Hawkins.

MANDY (*as* EVALINA *stands speechless, her mouth trembling*). Naw tain't all right, nuther. You go git dem dimes you is hid out, gal! You is been actin'-up all day. (*To* JIM.) I knows de signs! (*Seizing the hesitant* EVALINA *by the shoulder.*) You done laid dat money by fer a vain pu'pose—a on-righteous pu'pose!

EVALINA (*jerking away from* MANDY). I ain't got dat money. And I don't need it, *no*how! You and Jim Posey kin set up all de big heavy tombstones you wants, but I ain't sleepin' under none of 'em! (*Beginning to weep, she clings to the bed-post.*) I'se gwine sleep here in my *own* bed. (*Falling across the bed.*)

MANDY. You ain't sleepin' nowhere in dis house lessen you respects yo' deceased-ed husband!
(JIM *now strides to the front door, but pauses before* EVALINA *as she raises beseeching eyes to his.*)

JIM (*quietly looking down at her*). I'se steppin' out to de waggin a minute, Evalina. I got a use fer sumpum.

MANDY (*sternly to* EVALINA *as* JIM *hurries across the porch and down the steps*). You git up off dat quilt 'fo' you wrinkles up dem stars o' Bethlehem!

EVALINA (*rising and snatching the quilt from the bed*). Dis here yo' quilt, all right, but hit's my bed. (*Throwing the quilt on a chair and defiantly seating herself on the white sheets covering the mattress.*) I slep' on dis bed 'fo' ever I knowed Henry Hawkins, and I'se sleepin' on it atter I knows 'im! (EVALINA *rises hastily as she sees* JIM *entering hurriedly through the front door.* MANDY *shrinks back at the sight of the long-handled axe slung over* JIM'S *shoulder.*)

MANDY (*shrieking at* JIM *who is now skilfully taking the bed apart with the aid of the axe after having thrown mattress and pillows on the porch*). Whut you think you doin', upsettin' de house o' mo'ners dis-a-way!

JIM (*calmly disjoining the head of the bed from where he stands near the window, turns to* MANDY *with a wry grin*). I'se fixin' to find room (*Hammer.*) fer Evalina's (*Hammer.*) nex' restin' place, Miss Hawkins. (JIM *takes off the side-pieces of the bed now.*)

MANDY (*striding toward* EVALINA *as* JIM *carefully places the head-piece and the side-pieces on the porch outside.*) Is you fergittin' I done promise salvation fer you?

EVALINA (*clinging to the foot-piece of the bed to prevent its falling.*) I wants salvation while I'se *livin'!* Jes' lak I wants my *bow*-kays now, while I kin smell 'em! (*Scarcely noticing* JIM, *who takes the foot-piece from her and carries it to the porch.*) I ain't meanin' no disrespec' to you and Henry, Ma Hawkins (*weeping*) but—I—jes' nach'ly laks a warm bed!

MANDY. And who you think gwine save you on dat fearful resurrection day?

EVALINA (*simply, as her eyes turn to* JIM, *who has come inside*). I ain't gwine be skeerd wid Jim dere.

JIM. Git de rest o' dat beddin', Evalina. Us is fixin' to load de waggin, now. (*To* MANDY.) Us is settin' up dis bed in *my* house.

MANDY (*seizing her quilt*). You ain't haulin' dis quilt off in no waggin! (*To* EVALINA *who has gathered up the sheets from the floor*.) You a'n't takin' dem three dollars 'way fum here, nuther!

EVALINA (*as* JIM *relieves her of her burden and tosses the linens onto the porch*). Dem dimes was my winder-washin' money! (*Loosening her black skirt from the waist*.) But if I'se got to *prove* I ain't got 'em, *here's* what went wid 'em! (*Stepping out of her top skirt and standing boldly before* MANDY *in the full glory of scarlet satin*.)

MANDY (*her eyes bulging*). You—you—shameless— *widder!*

JIM (*taking* EVALINA *by the arm*). Don't you be worryin' 'bout no widder, Miss Hawkins. (*As they stand in the doorway, his arm about* EVALINA.) Nex' time you see Evalina, she gwine be rigged out in a *weddin'* dress!

EVALINA (*smiling up at* JIM). A red 'un?

JIM (*beaming down at her*). A red 'un what'll dazzle Miss Hawkins' eyes!

CURTAIN

THREE LINKS O' CHAIN

A PLAY OF NEGRO COUNTRY FOLK

Written in the playwriting course at the University of North Carolina and originally produced by The Carolina Playmakers on July 2, 1940.

THE CHARACTERS

MARY, *a Negress of southern Alabama*	Mary Stine
SKIP, *her husband*	Hoyt Bowen
MAGNOLIA, *their twelve-year-old daughter*	Lucy Bright Woodruff
LILY BELL } *their young twin daughters* {	Elizabeth Epple
LILY DEW } {	Catherine Porter Lewis
CA'LINE, *Mary's old mother*	Lillian Prince

SCENE: The front yard of Mary's cabin on the outskirts of Greenville, Alabama.

TIME: The present. A late afternoon in July.

THE SCENE

It is mid-afternoon of a July day. The warm sunshine, sifting through branches of sweet-gum and birch, weaves patterns of light and shade across the clean-swept dooryard of MARY MIDDLETON's *cabin. As the scene opens, the front of the small unpainted house, with mud chimney half hidden by clumps of lilac bushes, is visible at the left. The open door affords a glimpse of walls papered with magazines and newspapers, and crude furniture resting on the bare floor of the single "front room." At the right of the door an open shutter of boards reveals coarse lace curtains freshly-laundered and many-times mended. Outside, beneath the square opening of the window, is a shelf containing tin cans filled with geraniums. And on the ground, close to the house, is a flourishing border of bright "old-maids."*

At the rear, several feet to the right of the cabin which stands diagonally at the left, is an unpainted fence of uneven palings flanked by rows of vari-colored hollyhocks. A gate opens onto a path which leads through the pasture to the little ante-bellum town of Greenville, Alabama.

MARY, *a plump, ginger-colored Negress just past thirty, sits in the doorway and "unwrops" the woolly head of her daughter,* MAGNOLIA, *who is sprawled on the steps below her.* MARY's *own hair is neatly held in place by side-combs, bright green and studded with brilliants. There is a quality of softness about her round face and supple body, and her voice is mellow and tender. Like her* daughter, she is clad in starched, faded calico. Both darkies are barefooted. MARY wears a short white apron.

MAGNOLIA, a lanky brown-skinned girl of twelve, has no more grown to her awkward hands and feet than to her mother's old dress. Her broad smile and prominent white teeth give the impression of being grotesquely large for her inquisitive face.

Opposite the cabin, at the right, in the checkered shade of the tall poplar trees which enclose the yard, MARY's old mother, CA'LINE, is patiently preparing fruit for preserving. On the ground, at the left of her low hickory chair, is a pile of small green peaches, and an old dented pan. Nearby is a fifty-pound lard can of cold water into which she drops peach after peach after splitting it and removing the stone which she drops into a pan on her lap. At the right, in a large black wash-pot, ordinarily used for boiling clothes, other peaches are simmering. CA'LINE's fat black arms, bare to the elbow, move rhythmically. Years of toil have persuaded them to function automatically. Her flowered, rose calico dress is partially covered by an apron of China-blue chambray and she wears large brass rings in her ears. Her graying hair, evenly parted in small squares, is "wropped" in narrow strips of dark cloth which lie close to her head. On her broad feet are high-topped brogans.

LILY BELL, almost enveloped by one of CA'LINE's brown-checkered aprons tied around her neck, stands at the right of the steaming fruit. With a long, smooth paddle she lazily stirs the peaches in the black pot, watching MARY and MAGNOLIA the while. Facing the yard, LILY BELL's twin, LILY DEW, swings back and forth on the gate. The twins are dusky wide-eyed little girls with sturdy bodies, short for their nine years. Their crisp, red-

plaid ginghams are cut by the same pattern and each kinky mop is partially restrained by a pert bow of scarlet. LILY DEW's *finery, like* LILY BELL's, *is protected by one of* CA'LINE's *aprons. The feet of both children are bare.*

CA'LINE (*as* LILY BELL *gradually brings her slow, circular movements of the paddle to a stand-still*). You keep dem peaches stirrin', gal.
(LILY BELL *clasps the stick with both hands and moves it vigorously from one side of the pot to the other, almost losing her balance as her entire body sways with each swinging movement of her arms.*)

MARY. Stand back fum dat bilin' pot, Lily Bell.

LILY BELL (*seizing this opportunity to relax her efforts*). Is us gwine have peach 'zerves fer supper, Granny?

CA'LINE (*leaning to pick over the pile of fruit on the ground*). Ifn us don't, you'll eat dry hoe-cake. You chillun sopped up de last drap o' cane su'ip dis mawnin'.

LILY DEW (*climbing down from the gate on which she had been swinging, comes down to the lard can as* CA'LINE *drops a handful of fruit in the pan on her broad lap*). Cayn't us sop up de rest o' de sorghum, Granny? I'se tired o' hoe-cake and potlicker.

CA'LINE (*pointing to the steaming black pot*). Dat last jug o' sorghum's gwine be emptied in dem peaches. (*As she turns to* LILY DEW, LILY BELL *slips away from the pot and begins to play on the ground near the gate.*)

How you think I gwine make 'zerves widout no sweetnin'?

MAGNOLIA (*as* LILY DEW *joins* LILY BELL *to play in the sand*). What yawl worryin' 'bout sumpum t'eat tonight, fer? Ain't you gwine wait 'roun' at de church fer de weddin' supper?

CA'LINE (*contemptuously, turning to* MAGNOLIA). Weddin' supper!

MAGNOLIA. Dey's fo'teen tables settin' in de grove jes' outside de church. I counted 'em. Maybe Mr. Silas and his mule done hauled mo' tables to de churchyard by dis time. (*Smacking her lips.*) Mr. Silas say dem tables gwine be loaded down wid fixin's.

CA'LINE (*her eyes fixed on* MAGNOLIA). What you call yo'self doin', nosin' 'roun' a place lak dat?

MAGNOLIA (*loosening her hair from* MARY's *fingers and leaning forward, her hands on her knees*). Tain't no harm to nose 'roun' de churchyard, Granny. Not when you's pickin' blackberries, tain't.

LILY DEW (*looking up from where she is playing in the sand*). *Naw*, Granny. When you's huntin' berries, you kin go ever'where.

LILY BELL (*backing her sisters up*). Sho' kin—if you's got a bucket on yo' arm. Tain't nobody never run me home.

CA'LINE (*ignoring the twins and scowling at* MAGNOLIA). Blackberries! And hit de mont' o' *July*! Blackberries. Jew berries, Huckerberries. Dey's *been* gone.

MAGNOLIA. Hit's lak de twins say, Granny. Tain't no harm to jes' look fer berries.

CA'LINE. Ifn yo' ma listened to me lak she *oughter*, wouldn't none o' you chillun go nigh dat church today. Not fer dat weddin', you wouldn't.

MARY (*rising*). Aw now, Mama, us cayn't let Pinkie Sanders think she got us *plum* down. (*Thoughtfully, after a pause.*) Cose, if us all went to de weddin', Pinkie mought think us don't kere a-*tall*. But—

CA'LINE (*in a bored tone*). I knows. You done tole me dat by day, and you done tole me de same thing by night. (*Shaking her head slowly and mimicking the despairing* MARY.) You jes' cayn't stand to see yo' husband walk up and marry wid anudder 'oman. (MARY *takes a side-comb from her hair and begins to part the bushy mop of* MAGNOLIA *kneeling on the step beside her.*) Well, you ain't got no husband. And if you axes me, you ain't *had* none since Pinkie Sanders come back fum *De*-troit.

MARY (*hopelessly, as she absent-mindedly leaves her comb sticking in* MAGNOLIA's *hair*). Hit sho' look hard. (*Turning slightly to her cabin.*) And me wid a pair o' co't-house licenses hangin' right over my bed.

CA'LINE (*sighing and turning back to her peaches*). Yeh, Lawd. Hit sho' do look hard. Time was when a pair o' co't-house licenses meant sumpum. (*Wearily.*) But it ain't dat-a-way dese days.

(*Proudly adjusting the comb in her hair,* MAGNOLIA

flounces into the cabin followed by the admiring LILY
DEW. LILY BELL *continues to play in the sand.* MARY
walks listlessly toward CA'LINE, *seats herself, takes up
her knife and pan, and begins to seed the peaches. Suddenly she pauses, the fruit in her hand forgotten.*)

MARY. Dem two licenses is been framed and hangin' over de head-piece o' me and Skip's bed since de day us walked out dat co't-house.

CA'LINE. You had oughter hung dem licenses where Skip could see 'em. (*Philosophically.*) Tain't gwine do a man no harm to remind hisself, when he wakes up wid rangey notions in his head.

MARY (*happy for a moment in her memories*). Skip say dat mawnin' us walked out dat co't-house do', "Mary, some mens don't see no need fer dese licenses. But I'se proud to buy bofe of 'em fer you. But Mary," he say, "I ain't buyin' dese licenses fer you to bind me wid. I ain't gwine need no bindin'."

CA'LINE. Humph! You had oughter been walkin' out de church do', stid o' dat co't-house. Co't-houses ain't no fittin' place to marry.

MARY. You fergits hit was Jedge Baxter what married us, Mama. You know he's smart as air preacher what cayn't read and write.

CA'LINE. Dat ain't got nothin' to do wid it. Ifn 'twas Jedge Baxter or Jedge Ponty-yus Pilot, hit's all de same. Look a-here—you ain't never heerd tell o' no babtizin's and no buryin's in no co't-house, is you? De Lawd ain't made co't-houses fer sech. And he ain't made 'em to marry in, nuther. Dey's too close to de jailhouse. (*Laying her knife in her lap.*) Jedge Baxter's been a mighty good friend to white *and* black. And I ain't sayin' he ain't yo' friend, yit. But when hit come to marryin' folks fer now and eternal, he's done overstretched his power.

MARY. My co't-house licenses looks de same as folks' what promises in de church, Mama—ifn I did run away to marry. (*Anxiously.*) You ain't skeerd my licenses ain't ... lawful ... is you? (CA'LINE *is obviously noncommittal.*) You don't think Skip run off 'cause he ain't bound to us, does you?

CA'LINE. Bound or no bound, Skip's done left you fer dat Pinkie Sanders. And he's followin' Pinkie back to *De*-troit tonight—ifn she buy 'im dat railroad ticket lak Silas say.

MARY. Silas say he givin' Skip dat divorce fer choppin' his cotton.

CA'LINE. Dem law papers is de onliest way dat jack-leg lawyer kin pay anybody. But folks oughter have mo' gumption dan to tech dem trouble-makin' papers. Dem's de devil's instru*mints*. And dem's devil's wages Skip's collectin'.

MARY (*sorrowfully*). Skip chopped cotton a whole mont' fer dat divorce. (*Suddenly hopeful.*) But Skip ain't played his *git*-tar to nair 'oman but me. Folks say he ain't sung to no other 'oman, nuther.

CA'LINE. *Git*-tars don't whine out no promises. Dey *sounds* good, but— Whar dey led *you?*

MARY. Miss Lucretia say a pair o' co't-house licenses binds a man to you—if you buys 'em lawful, in de beginnin', she say.

CA'LINE. How she know? Ain't none o' her mens bought her no licenses.

MARY. Dat's so. (*Suddenly, after a pause.*) But maybe she don't need no law. She a cunjer-'oman. (*At the word "cunjer" LILY BELL rises and begins to listen attentively as she takes a position between MARY and CA'LINE.*)

CA'LINE (*impatiently*). If she a cunjer-'oman, why ain't she cunjered up sumpum 'sides dat monkey-face Silas she been a-takin' on wid? If she a cunjer-'oman, why ain't she found out Silas is a jack-leg lawyer lak Jedge Baxter done warn Skip?

MARY (*dismissing the riddle as though it were beyond human interpretation*). I dunno. Miss Lucretia say she kin tell a 'oman how to put a spell on a man any time, do'—if she wanter.

CA'LINE. A 'oman's got to put her own spell on her own man. Lucretia ain't gwine tell 'er how—if she ever knowed how. (*Confidentially, after a brief silence.*) Tain't allus safe to turn yo' man over to no sho'-nuff cunjer-'oman, nuther.

LILY BELL (*beginning to stir the fruit once more after slyly licking the stick*). De preacher say Miss Lucretia puts spells on folks.

CA'LINE. Dat preacher wouldn't know what a spell was. (*Laughing softly to herself.*) If he ever knowed, he's done fergot. He's old, dat preacher is.

LILY BELL. Don't you even b'lieve in signs lak screech owls, Granny?

CA'LINE (*as* MAGNOLIA *returns to the doorway of the cabin, a crude mirror in her hand*). Screech owls and sech is God's critters—if dey *is* bad luck. Lucretia ain't no critter. She jes' a sinful 'oman. She b'longs to de devil—if she b'longs to any man.

MAGNOLIA (*standing propped against the doorway*). Miss Pinkie Sanders is got a spell what works. I heerd Mr. Silas talkin' 'bout it dis mawnin'.

CA'LINE. Dat yaller Silas ain't been tryin' to git sassy wid you, is he?

MAGNOLIA. Nawm, he ain't seed me. I was pickin' blackberries (*As* CA'LINE *gives her a menacing look.*)— lookin' fer 'em, I means—up back o' de church.

MARY (*anxiously, as* MAGNOLIA *seats herself on the steps to primp in the mirror*). And whar was *Silas*?

MAGNOLIA. Him and de mule was in de grove wid Miss Lucretia. She was spreadin' white cloths on de tables what Mr. Silas and de mule brung over on dey waggin.

CA'LINE (*reasoning to herself*). Fo'teen tables and fo'teen white tablecloths. I wonder is dat what dat brassy Lucretia wanted wid my white tablecloth? She better not be done borried it fer dat Pinkie Sanders! (*Turning to* MAGNOLIA.) Did you see my Sunday tablecloth on air one o' dem tables, Macknolia?

MAGNOLIA. Nawm. I never seed nothin' dat close. But I heerd a plenty.

LILY BELL (*running toward* MAGNOLIA). Tell us 'bout Miss Pinkie's spell, Magnolia! Was hit a cunjer spell?

CA'LINE. You come back to dis pot! Fus' thing you knows, I gwine cunjer you wid dat stick. (*Pointing to the paddle in the pot.*)

MARY (*rising*). I'll stir de 'zerves, Mama. I reckon she tired. (LILY BELL *sinks down on the steps and gazes up at* MAGNOLIA.)

MAGNOLIA (*importantly, as she looks into* LILY BELL'S *inquiring eyes*). Dis spell were a love charm.

LILY BELL. A love charm?

MAGNOLIA. Yeh, Mr. Silas say Miss Pinkie done worked it on a heap o' mens 'fo' she worked it on our pappy. (*Giggling.*) Mr. Silas say she been tryin' to work it on him, too.

CA'LINE (*nodding to* MARY). Mmn-humn! (*Turning to* MAGNOLIA.) And what did Lucretia say to dat?

MAGNOLIA. Miss Lucretia, she got mad. So mad she jerk de tablecloth right out Mr. Silas's hand. And him a-helpin' 'er spread it. Served 'er right, de cloth tore smack in two.

CA'LINE. Dat better not be my tablecloth!

MAGNOLIA (*enjoying the attention of her audience*). Mr. Silas, he say Miss Pinkie totes a bottle o' love medicine.

LILY BELL. Does you drink hit?

MAGNOLIA. Naw, tain't nothin' fer yo' insides.

MARY (*looking up from her stirring*). Must be a lini*mint*.

LILY BELL (*curiously, as* MAGNOLIA *consciously withholds her secret*). Was Mr. Silas skeerd to rub de lini*mint* on hisself?—Does hit burn?

MAGNOLIA (*innocently*). I reckon hit must burn. Mr. Silas say hit got fire in hit. He say hit done burnt up our pappy.

MARY (*to* CA'LINE). Must-a been sumpum lak Hi-Life. (*Suddenly vehement, she goes toward* MAGNOLIA *who rises at her approach.*) You mean to say yo' pappy never had no mo' sense dan to rub dat fiery hoss lini*mint* on hisself? Macknolia, you is fibbin'!

MAGNOLIA. Nawm I ain't. And I ain't said my pappy rubbed nothin' on hisself. (*Pouting as she turns away and mutters to herself.*) And not on no hoss and no mule, nuther.

MARY. What he done wid it, den?

MAGNOLIA. Mr. Silas say my pappy put hit on Miss Pinkie Sanders. Say dat's de way de love charm work! (*Rubbing her hands over her shoulders, arms, and thighs.*) Say if you kin put dat linimint all over yo' gal, she yorn.

LILY BELL (*rising to stare up into* MAGNOLIA's *face*). Jes' lak dey say you kin ketch a bird ifn you puts salt on hit's tail?

MAGNOLIA. Naw, tain't lak dat. Birds flys off. I done tried salt. But Miss Lucretia, she never run off. Naw sir! Stood right dere. Atter Mr. Silas unstopped dat bottle, too!

CA'LINE. And I reckon you "stood right dere" and watched dat Lucretia git liniminted.

MAGNOLIA (*simply, as she takes up her mirror and sits on the steps*). Miss Lucretia never got rubbed. (LILY BELL *sits beside her.*) Mr. Silas say Miss Pinkie give 'im dat linimint to use on *her*. Say hit smell sweet jes' lak Miss Pinkie do. Say he aimin' to use hit lak she *say*—when my pappy ain't 'roun'. (*After a pause, turning from the mirror, as* CA'LINE *and* MARY *exchange meaningful glances.*) I wisht I had some o' dat sweet-smellin' linimint.

CA'LINE. You better stay fum behind dat church, 'fo' you finds sumpum you ain't got no business wid.

MARY (*thinking aloud*). I wisht I knowed what was in dat lini*mint*. (*Appealing to* CA'LINE.) Mama, you's good at stewin' up herbs and things.

CA'LINE. I makes my tonics and lini*mints* fer ail*mints*. I ain't never had to fall back on tricks fer *my* lovin'.

LILY BELL. My pappy say you sho' stirs up a pow'ful leaf brew.

MAGNOLIA. When Miss Lucretia come atter dat tonic she call 'erself got de dye-sentry.

LILY BELL (*admiringly*). She fancy!

CA'LINE (*abruptly*). Fancy ladies don't have no good name.

MARY (*becoming aware of the crude playing of a guitar indoors*). Dat twin's done got Skip's *git*-tar! (*Going toward the house.*) You Lily Dew! You put dat *git*-tar down! (*Pulling the curtains apart and peering inside.*) You climb up dat ladder and put dat *git*-tar back in de loft! (*Turning to* CA'LINE.) I might-a knowed she was up to sumpum. (*Thrusting her head in the window.*) Don't you drap Skip's instru*mint!* Dat's right. Come on down fum dere, now.

CA'LINE (*as* MARY *turns from the window and comes down in front of the steps*). Hit's queer Skip ain't been atter his *git*-tar. I ain't never knowed 'im to be widout it.

MARY (*reminiscently*). He useter strum on hit ever' night. Day time, too, heap o' days. (*Her face lighting up.*) "Mary," he allus say, "when I'se happy, I has to make music!" (*Turning to* CA'LINE.) Sometimes, when I teches dat *git*-tar, I feels a hope in my heart. (*Forgetting* CA'LINE *and the children.*) When I slips up in de loft and takes hit in my arms, seems lak I'm holdin' Skip close. (*Softly.*) And de sound o' de strings is like ... like Skip ... a-whisperin' to me.

CA'LINE (*unromantically*). Pinkie Sanders ain't got nothin' on Skip when hit comes to love charms. I dunno what Skip's worked on Pinkie; but he's sho' worked a charm on you wid dat *git*-tar.
(LILY DEW *darts from behind the far side of the house and, sniffing, goes to the simmering fruit.*)

MARY (*taking no notice of* LILY DEW *who is now bending far over the steaming pot*). I reckon dey ain't no 'oman kin hold out agin Skip when he sing and play. Does yawl recollect how he useter sing "Three Links o' Chain"?

LILY DEW (*standing up straight*). *I* does!

MARY. He say you chillun was de three links o' *his* chain.

LILY BELL. And us dance all 'roun' you and him when he sung dat song. Us jine hands and make a chain!

CA'LINE (*sorrowfully*). Dey ain't no love chain.
(*As* LILY BELL *demonstrates how the children dance to the music of* SKIP's *voice and guitar,* MAGNOLIA *sneaks over to the heap of fruit.*)

THREE LINKS O' CHAIN 49

LILY DEW (*singing*).

Sis-ter Ma-ry had three links o' chain.

MARY (*hysterically*). Shet up!
(CA'LINE *turns just in time to see* MAGNOLIA *snatch a peach from the pile beside her chair.*)

CA'LINE (*giving* MAGNOLIA *a forceful push*). You git away fum dese peaches!

MARY (*seeing* MAGNOLIA *cram the peach, seed and all, into her mouth*). Take dat wormy green peach out yo' mouf, Macknolia!

CA'LINE (*rising hastily*). I thought dem peaches was dwindlin' mighty fast! (*As* CA'LINE *comes toward her,* MAGNOLIA *places her hand over her bulging jaw. Gulping, she skips about the yard.* CA'LINE *seizes her by the shoulder and she seems to swallow the peach.*)

CA'LINE (*stepping back as* MAGNOLIA *takes her hand from her mouth*). You jes' wait till you gits rid o' dat seed you done swallowed. I'se gwine frail you till you cayn't set on a fedder-bed!

MARY (*quietly*). Go on in de house and git yo' shoes on, Macknolia. Hit's most time to go to de church.

CA'LINE (*turning quickly to* MARY). Is you done lost all yo' senses over Skip? You know Macknolia ain't had shoes on her feets since she scuffed out dem brogans playin' jump-rope.

MAGNOLIA (*triumphantly, taking a step toward* CA'LINE). My mama gwine lend me her shoes.

CA'LINE (*her eyes following* MAGNOLIA *who is prancing toward the house*). I bet her black belly is so full o' peaches, her insides is fuzzy!
(MARY *drops a seeded peach in the can as she looks up to see* LILY DEW *licking the syrupy end of the paddle. The twins have taken advantage of their elders, lifting the dripping paddle from the syrup and licking it by turns.*)

MARY. You put dat stick back in dat pot! Lily Dew, hit's yo' turn to stir. Lily Bell, you go take yo' seat on dem do' steps till I tells you to git up!

MAGNOLIA (*thrusting her head out the window as* LILY BELL *moves reluctantly toward the steps*). If my insides is fuzzy, yo's is stuck together. (*She sticks out her tongue at* LILY BELL *before drawing the curtains.*)

CA'LINE (*as* LILY BELL *seats herself*). Lily Bell, you git up fum dere and bring me dat jug o' sorghum. (*As* LILY BELL *goes into the cabin.*) And don't you drink none, nuther! (*Stirring the peaches vigorously.*) Macknolia, you come on out dat house 'fo' you starts meddlin' wid my things!
(*Almost immediately* MAGNOLIA *comes down the steps, her awkward feet cramped in* MARY'S *high-heeled, patent-leather shoes.*)

CA'LINE. Jes' look a-dere, Mary. We ain't saved nothin' by lettin' dat gal run barefooted. Her feets is big as her pappy's.

MAGNOLIA (*hopefully, sitting on the steps and looking at her outstretched feet*). We could split dese slippers.

CA'LINE (*contemptuously*). Dat's one nigger trick I don't do. Hit's plum foolish crampin' up yo' feets lak dey was little, and den splittin' yo' shoes 'cross de toes so you kin walk.

MAGNOLIA. Hit's a good trick, Granny. All de colored folks does it. White folks is done took to it, too.

LILY DEW (*whirling about the yard, her skirts and apron flying*). Sho' is. Ever'body wears dey toes out, now. Sandals, dey calls dem cut-out shoes.

CA'LINE. Split 'em, if you wanter. But you ain't cuttin' up *my* shoes. I ain't carin' *what* sto' man knows how big *my* feets is. (*Muttering to herself as she looks at the fruit-juice dripping from the paddle she holds high over the pot, while* MARY *stoops to feel* MAGNOLIA's *toes inside the tight slippers.*) Tain't no man's business, lessen hit's de Lawd's. Tain't nothin' 'bout me no man's business. I'se a widder 'oman, I is!
(MARY *picks up her knife and makes a small slit on the outer side of each shoe.* LILY BELL *comes out of the house with the jug.*)

CA'LINE (*after tasting the syrup on the paddle*). Hit's ready. Pour de sorghum in. (LILY BELL *holds back some of the sorghum.*) Pour hit all in. Hit goes fudder dis-a-way. (LILY BELL *turns the jug upside-down.*) Dat's hit. Now. (*To* LILY DEW *who is dancing about the pot.*) You pick up dem pans and put 'em in dat lard can. (*Handing the jug back to* LILY BELL *after shaking it over the pot.*) Go put dis back in de kitchen.

MAGNOLIA (*jumping up from the steps*). Dese shoes feels good enough to dance in, now.

CA'LINE. Ain't nobody gwine dance at dat weddin'.

MARY (*going to relieve* LILY DEW *who is picking up the peach pits she has spilled from the pans*). Go 'roun' to de well now and wash yo' hands, Lily Dew. (LILY DEW *skips back of the house.*) Mama, I wisht you would go 'long wid de chillun. Dey need you.

CA'LINE (*emphatically*). I ain't never went to no devil doin's. And I ain't startin' now.

MARY (*to* MAGNOLIA, *as* LILY BELL *comes out of the house*). Untie Lily Bell's ap'on, Macknolia.

CA'LINE (*stooping to pick up scattered seeds as* MAGNOLIA *jerks off* LILY BELL'S *apron and tosses it indoors*). Dis is de fus' time ever I seed sech. (*Rising.*) I'se heerd o' chillun goin' to dey mammy's weddin' 'fo' dey was bawn, (*Shaking her head disapprovingly.*) but I ain't never heerd o' women sendin' *proper* chillun to dey own pappy's weddin'.

MAGNOLIA (*drawing* LILY BELL *along with her, as she moves toward the gate*). Anyhow, de preacher say we ain't no wood's-colt chillun, if our mammy did run away.

LILY DEW (*bobbing up from outside the fence*). Come on, yawl! We gwine be late fer de weddin'!

MARY. Wait dere, Lily Dew! What you got in dat bundle?

LILY DEW (*trying to conceal something behind her full skirt*). Hit's jes' a weddin' present fer my pappy.

CA'LINE. You come back hyar! (*Seizing* LILY DEW *from across the fence.*) Hand me dat thing! (LILY DEW *guiltily hands her burden over the fence and the blue-checkered apron in which it was wrapped falls on the palings.* MARY *starts at the sight of* SKIP's *guitar.*)

CA'LINE. What you think you doin', sneakin' out lak dis?

LILY DEW (*shrieking*). Dat's my pappy's *git*-tar! I wants 'im to make music fer me!

CA'LINE (*laying the guitar on her chair*). If yo' pappy wants dis, he kin come git it! (*Turning back to* LILY DEW *who has begun to cry softly.*) I had oughter whup you!

MARY. Don't, Mama. She ain't done nothin'! She ... she love Skip's music ... same as I does.

CA'LINE (*softening, she gazes at the whimpering* LILY DEW, *and pushes* LILY BELL *toward the gate*). Go 'long, all o' you! (*Removing her apron and hanging it on the fence.*) Hush dat snifflin', Lily Dew!

MARY (*in surprise, as* CA'LINE *goes to follow the children*). Is you gwine to de weddin', Mama?

CA'LINE. Weddin' nothin'! I'se gwine atter my tablecloth!

MAGNOLIA (*calling as they all march off right*). I'se gwine bring you a sweet-pertater pie, Mama!

LILY BELL. Me too!

LILY DEW (*coming back to lean over the fence*). I'se gwine slip you a heap o' good things, Mama!

CA'LINE (*Moving out of sight*). Come on, yawl. (*Her voice receding in the distance as* LILY DEW *climbs down from the fence and scampers away.*) You got to *run* if you keeps up wid *me*.
(*After watching them down the road,* MARY *turns from the fence. She takes up a stick and rakes the fire from under the pot of peaches. As she starts wearily to the cabin she stoops down to touch* SKIP's *guitar lovingly. Nearing the door, she stops suddenly as she hears footsteps.* SKIP, *a powerful, brown-skinned darkie in a brown-checkered suit, starched white shirt, and gay bow-tie, comes to the gate from the left. He wears a red geranium in the lapel of his coat but his unhappy countenance is not in keeping with his wedding finery.*)

SKIP (*softly, his hands clenched over the pickets of the gate*). Mary? (MARY *does not answer, but after a moment of hesitation,* SKIP *comes into the yard.*)

MARY (*pointing to the guitar on the chair*). Dere 'tis. (SKIP *stands gazing down at the guitar.*)

MARY. Go on and take hit. Lily Dew would-a brung hit to de church, but—

SKIP. I knows, Mary. (*Pointing off left.*) I been waitin' out yonder till dey all left you.

MARY (*looking sorrowfully at the guitar*). Hit's yourn, Skip. I reckon I had oughter made 'em take hit to you.

SKIP. I ain't axed de chillun to bring hit to me, Mary. (*Lowering his head.*) I ... I ain't been ... wantin' hit.

MARY. But you's come fer it, now.

SKIP (*defenselessly, as he raises his eyes*). I'se hungry fer it, Mary. Fer a long time I ain't had de heart to play it, but ... (*Lifting the instrument, he holds it to him as though it were his only solace. Appealing to* MARY, *he takes a step toward her.*) You know I cayn't live widout music, Mary. (*He looks down at the guitar and finds its appeal irresistible. He strums a chord or two.* MARY *goes to the steps and sits down, covering her face with her hands.*)

MARY (*her back to him*). Don't, Skip. . . .

SKIP. What's de matter, Mary? (*Taking another step toward her.*) Don't you lak my music no mo'? (*She does not answer.*) I don't blame you fer hatin' me, Mary. But you allus useter ... want me to ... (*Break-

ing off helplessly.) You allus loved my music same as I did, Mary.

MARY (*raising her eyes to his own*). I loves hit now, Skip. De sound o' dem strings is like you a-talkin'. But hit useter be me yo' music talked to. (*As she gets up to go indoors.*) I don't want to hear it ... now. ...

SKIP (*coming to the steps*). Mary! (*She turns at the door.*) I know you ain't wantin' me here, but I ... I had to tell you. Mary, de devil's had me. (*His foot on the step; she stands looking down at him.*) But my music ... de devil ain't give me dat. God give hit to me. (*Hugging the guitar close.*) I knows hit now, 'cause I couldn't sing when de devil had me.

MARY (*hesitant*). You ain't sung to ... Pinkie?

SKIP (*dropping his head*). I been drinkin' a heap, Mary. When Pinkie say "Sing," I laugh and say I don't wanter. I couldn't sing. Dis mawnin', I got sick o' Pinkie and her liquor and I went down to de spring (*Taking her hand as she turns from him.*)—de spring where you useter meet me, Mary. (*Leaning the guitar beside the house and drawing her down on the steps, he sits at her feet.*) Dat clear, fresh water God made tasted sweet. Hit brung back remembrance o' you. And hit ... hit cleansed me ... lak de preacher say babtizin' water kin.

MARY. I'm glad it holp you, Skip.

SKIP. I seen yo' face in de spring same I useter, when you leaned over and we drunk together. (*After a silence.*) Dat water quench my thirst. But I got hongrier and hongrier fer my music. I was 'shamed to talk to de Lawd—but I *had* to. I called on Him, and He . . . He answered me.

MARY (*her hand closing over his*). Co'se He did, Skip.

SKIP (*joyously*). He let me lift up my voice and sing. (*Softly.*) But I was singin' to you.
(*As* MARY *smiles down at him,* MAGNOLIA *and the twins come bounding along from the right.*)

MAGNOLIA (*breathlessly coming through the gate, stopping just inside*). Ever'body comin' 'way fum de church! (*Her eyes rolling.*) Miss Pinkie Sanders is done run off wid Mr. Silas and de love charm!

LILY DEW. Dey gone to *De*-troit! Tain't gwine be no weddin'!

LILY BELL (*pouting*). And no weddin' supper, nuther.

MAGNOLIA. De ladies is done drug off dey tablecloths wid all de fixin's! Dey's totin' all de victuals home in dem white cloths.

LILY BELL (*joyously, as* MAGNOLIA *and* LILY DEW *realize the presence of their father and crowd around him*). Goody! Goody! Pappy's come home! (LILY BELL *runs into his outstretched arms.*)

LILY DEW (*picking up the guitar*). Here yo' *git*-tar, Pappy. (*Clutching it to her small breast before hand-*

ing it to him.) You kin make all de music you wanter now.

CA'LINE (*rushing in from the right*). Dat Lucretia thought she *better* bring dis cloth back loaded. (*Coming through the gate and depositing the feast near the chair.*) Us ain't gwine eat no mo' hoe-cake dis day—not fer days to come, nuther!

MAGNOLIA (*inspecting the contents of the tablecloth*). Miss Lucretia sho' jerked off plenty o' fixin's wid dis cloth!

CA'LINE. She skeerd not to. (*Seeing* SKIP *as she turns from all the children who have crowded about the food.*) What *you* doin', here? If you wants comp'ny, you kin foller dat Pinkie and Silas off to *De*-troit!

LILY DEW (*turning from the feast to defend her father*). My pappy come atter his *git*-tar!

CA'LINE. Let 'im take his box and *git*, den!

SKIP. I'm goin', Miss Ca'line. But if I had a-wanted to go wid Pinkie, I'd a-gone on dat ticket to *De*-troit what she bought me.

CA'LINE (*her hands on her hips*). I reckon Pinkie left off de price o' de weddin' licenses. If you'd a-had dem, I bet you'd be off marryin' wid Pinkie now!

SKIP (*calmly*). Hit's Silas what's gwine finish up dat job fer me. I give him de ticket to *De*-troit.

CA'LINE. You ain't got dem two dollars fer dem co't-house licenses. Dat's how 'tis.

SKIP (*standing his guitar beside the steps*). Nawm, I ain't got no two dollars, now. But I had 'em. (*Drawing two marriage licenses from his pocket.*) I done spent 'em on dese here. (*Going to* MARY *who is standing near the window.*) Jedge Baxter fixed up me and you some fresh licenses, Mary. (*Clasping her hand.*) I ain't axin' you to take me back, now. But I... I had to blot out dat divo'ce. Hit's a ugly thing, Mary. Here, honey. (*Forcing the papers into* MARY'S *hands.*) If you'll take dese, I'll git some purty frames fer 'em.

MARY (*shyly*). Co't-house licenses ain't no use, lessen you marries wid 'em.

SKIP (*seizing both her hands*). Mary, if you kin fergive me— Let's go up to de church and make dese licenses good!

CA'LINE (MAGNOLIA *goes to take the curtains from the window*). You better hang dem licenses over de *foot* o' yo' bed dis time!

LILY DEW (*gleefully*). Mama's gwine be de bride! (*She goes to pick the hollyhocks by the fence.* LILY BELL *runs to help her.*)

MAGNOLIA (*draping the lace curtains on* MARY *as a bridal veil*). Come on, Granny, help me!

CA'LINE (*relenting*). I had oughter been dere to fix you up proper de fus' time. (*As the beaming* MARY *turns to her.*) I'd a-seen it done right.

(Mary, *standing between* Magnolia *and* Ca'line, *unties her apron and tosses it through the doorway of the cabin.* Magnolia, *with the assistance of* Ca'line, *and the comb and pins from her own hair, fastens the lace to* Mary's *hair.*)

Magnolia. Dat church sho' is decorated up! I bet de folks'll be glad to bring de supper back. (*Looking up as she kneels to pin the curtains together near the hem.*) Dey's been countin' on dat party. (Magnolia *removes her shoes and places them on* Mary's *feet.*)

Skip. You sho' looks good to me, Mary. (*Chuckling as he stands admiring her.*) Purtier dan you looked de fus' time.
(Mary, *grinning happily, looks back at* Skip *and prances to the center of the yard. As the twins fill her arms with hollyhocks she turns her eyes from* Skip's *to beam on the children and the bridal bouquet.*)

Ca'line (*proudly*). Dis here's gwine be a proper weddin'! (*Adjusting* Mary's *train.*) My gal's a sho' nuff bride, now. Gwine be married in de church (*Punctuating each pleat she makes of the lace with her phrases.*)—wid a preacher—in de sight o' de Lawd—and her *mammy!*

Ca'line (Skip *takes up his guitar and steps to* Mary's *side*). Come here, Lily Dew and Lily Bell, and tote de train.
(Mary *takes* Skip's *arm and the twins lift the long train. To the tune of "Sister Mary Had Three Links o' Chain," strummed on the guitar by* Skip, *and sung by all, the joyous procession forms. Circling the entire*

WOOTTEN–MOULTON

THREE LINKS O' CHAIN

Sis-ter Ma-ry had three links o' chain.

yard, the smiling couple, followed by the twins who "tote" the train and MAGNOLIA with CA'LINE at her left, marches through the gate and off right toward the church. The children and CA'LINE prance and shuffle as they keep time to the music which is sung and played with increasing lustiness. Just after CA'LINE drops back of MAGNOLIA to pass through the gate, she runs back into the yard and gathers up the cloth laden with good things. Still singing, she hurries to bring up the rear of the procession as SKIP and MARY march off right.)

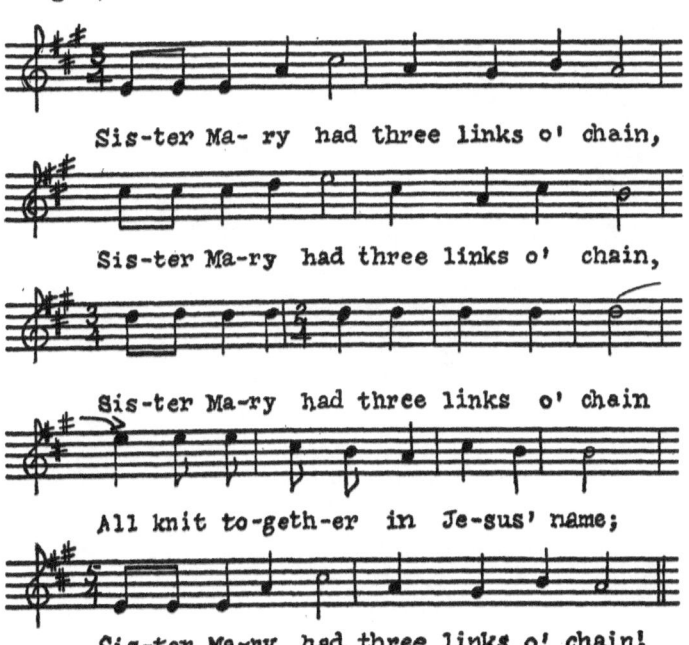

Sis-ter Ma-ry had three links o' chain,

Sis-ter Ma-ry had three links o' chain,

Sis-ter Ma-ry had three links o' chain

All knit to-geth-er in Je-sus' name;

Sis-ter Ma-ry had three links o' chain!

CURTAIN

WATERMELON TIME

A COMEDY OF THE BLACK BELT

Written in the playwriting course at the University of North Carolina and originally produced by The Carolina Playmakers, May 30, 1940.

THE CHARACTERS

GINSIE, *president of "The Daughters of Holiness"*
  Margaret Holmes
JAKE, *her husband* — Douglas Watson
NAZARENE, *their daughter* — Rae Murden
GERANIUM, *Ginsie's niece* — Frances Goforth
ALECK, *Geranium's admirer* — Howard Richardson
THE PARSON — Richard Porter Lewis

SCENE: The front yard of Ginsie's cabin on the outskirts of Tuscaloosa, Alabama.

TIME: The present. Mid-afternoon of an April day.

THE SCENE

It is mid-afternoon of an April day. An unpainted cabin, shaded by tall poplar trees rising from the edge of a dense ravine at the rear, stands in the center of a yard bare of grass. The plain board door in the center of the cabin front is flanked by wooden window shutters. Beneath the closed shutters are crude flower shelves. Steps scrubbed clean lead to the closed cabin door. Gay petunias flourish in front of the cabin, and on each side of the door step are beds of purple and red verbena bordered with inverted bottles of alternating brown and green glass thrust into the hard baked ground.

Near the flower beds are a number of plants in unpainted tin cans of various sizes which have evidently been removed from the shelves to be watered. A clothesline stretches from the corner of the cabin to the chinaberry trees at the right, a man's freshly-laundered white shirt hanging on it. Under the chinaberry trees is a washbench on which rest two wooden tubs. A huge black wash-pot stands over a bed of ashes on the opposite side of the yard. To the left are twin live oaks with a plank nailed between to form a seat.

As the scene opens, GINSIE, *a large black woman of about fifty, dressed in bright calico, is standing behind the wash-bench vigorously rubbing out linens in a tub of soapy water.* GERANIUM, *a young ginger-colored girl in a ruffly gay-flowered print which contrasts oddly with the blue-checkered apron she is wearing, is seated on the steps applying "anti-kink" to her hair. A small mirror stands upright on the steps beside her.*

GINSIE (*looks up as she wrings out a sheet, about to drop it into a tub of clear water*). How-come you got to go apin' white folks, Geranium? Ain't I done told you 'bout usin' dat hair-straightenin'?

GERANIUM (*reluctantly putting down the bottle of hair tonic on the step*). My hair ain't meant to be kinky, Aunt Ginsie. My pa, he say—

GINSIE (*dropping the sheet in the tub of rinsing water*). Don't come at me 'bout yo' pa! He done left Alabama fer good, lessen he aimin' to spend de balance o' his days in de jail-house. (*Lifting other linens from the suds, wringing each piece before dropping it into the clear water.*) Geranium, you is Viney's gal, and she my sister, and she my color.

GERANIUM (*looking away sullenly*). My gran'pa, he—

GINSIE (*her arms akimbo, her capable hands on her fat hips*). Yeh, I reckon you done heerd 'bout *him*, too. I reckon yo' pa done stuffed you full o' notions 'bout his pa what was white. Well, you ain't never had no gran'pa. (*Turning back to her clothes.*) Not on yo' pa's side, you ain't. (*She begins to souse the linens up and down in the rinsing tub, muttering half to* GERANIUM, *half to herself.*) Leastwise yo' gran'pa wa'n't no fambly man. (*Vehemently.*) And anyhow, ifn he had a-been, he knocked at back do's same as niggers! (GINSIE *wrings another sheet and hangs it on the line.* GERA-

NIUM *seizes this opportunity to apply more "anti-kink" to her hair.*)

GERANIUM (*proudly*). My gran'pa were a *in*-shawnce man.

GINSIE (*fastening other linens to the line with clothes pins*). Ain't no white mens had no dealin's wid 'im. And you listen to dis, Geranium! (*Her shoulders thrown back, her generous waist thrust forward aggressively as she confronts her niece.*) Ain't no 'spectable man goes knockin' at white folks' back do's lessen he a nigger!
(GERANIUM *realizes that* GINSIE *is staring at her hair which is now standing out from her head like flattened wires. She puts the bottle down guiltily.*)

GINSIE. You come stick yo' head in dis here wash-pot. (GERANIUM *shrinks back, shielding her head with her hands as* GINSIE *comes toward her.*) You hears me! (*Seizing* GERANIUM *by the shoulder and jerking her up from the steps.*) What you think de pahson gwine think dis ev'nin' ifn he come here and find a porkypine on my do' steps?

GERANIUM (*shrieking as* GINSIE *draws her down to the wash-pot*). Hit's got lye in hit!

GINSIE. I reckon lye won't hurt *you* none. (*She tests the water with her hand and forces* GERANIUM's *limp body over the wash-pot.*) Fus' thing you knows (*Rubbing* GERANIUM's *head vigorously.*) de church-folks'll be waitin' on you. Dey'll be tellin' me you is gallivantin' lak yo' ma. But not ifn it's none o' *my* business, you ain't!

GERANIUM (*struggling*). Ouch, Aunt Ginsie! Dis lye burn!

GINSIE (*rubbing* GERANIUM'S *head harder*). Lawd, sometimes I think de pahson oughter sprinkle lye in de water when he babtizes some o' dese folks 'roun' here. (*She draws* GERANIUM *out of the pot by the nap of her black woolly head.*)*

GINSIE. Dere, now. (*As* GERANIUM *shakes the water from her naturally short, kinky hair.*) What I done told you? Yo' hair de same as me and Viney's. (GERANIUM, *pouting sullenly, goes to the steps and sits down.*) And long as Viney leaves you on my hands, I'se gwine bring you up 'spectable same as I brung up Nazarene.

GERANIUM (*gazing at her reflection in the small mirror beside the bottle of hair-tonic*). Well, anyhow, I ain't no blacker'n snuff. I ain't *sut*-black lak Nazarene.

GINSIE (*raking ashes from beneath the pot with a stick of firewood*). And you ain't some 'count lak Nazarene, nuther! Hadn't a-been fer yo' ways. Nazarene would a-been here helpin' me now. (*As* GERANIUM *puts down her mirror and rises sullenly.*) She'd a-done had all Miss Mary's clothes washed and iron and toted home.

---

* This change may be effected by having GERANIUM, during the shampoo, exchange the tonic-soaked wig for one of kinky Negro hair.

(*Coming back toward the doorway.*) We'd a-done been ready fer de pahson, too! (*Prizing open the left window shutter with some difficulty and giving* GERANIUM, *who stands marking the ground with a toe of her shoe, a look of disgust.*) Go yonder and git dem washtubs offen dat bench. Empty 'em on dem hydrangies by de ravine. (*Opening the shutter and peering inside the cabin.*) *You* Jake! You git outten dat bed! You know dat pahson gwine be here dis ev'nin' to babtize you! (*Closing the shutter and turning to* GERANIUM *who comes forward after lifting the tubs from the bench and dragging them behind the sheets on the clotheslines.*) I'se been a-workin' on Jake 'bout dis babtizin' most ever' Sad-dy night us been married.

GERANIUM. Wouldn't Unker Jake ruther be babtized at de big meetin' in de mawnin', Aunt Ginsie?

GINSIE (*taking a small shovel from beside the house and scraping up the ashes and small sticks that were under the wash pot*). I ain't takin' no mo' chances on Sad-dy nights, Geranium. Co'se now, I ruther Jake go 'fo' de church-folks and 'pent o' he sins, and be babtized on a Sabbath lak a Christian oughter, (*Rising with effort.*) but I done told de pahson to come here on a Sad-dy. (*With spirit*). And I done told 'im to come 'fo' dark, too! (*Crossing to right and handing the shovel to* GERANIUM. Empty dese here ashes in de can. (*As* GERANIUM *goes back of the house* GINSIE *surveys the ground and stops, mumbling.*) Chicken fedders done blowed all over dis place. Well, pahson ain't gwine kere, I reckon—not when he see de table I done sot fer he supper, he ain't.

GERANIUM (*coming from around the side of the house as* GINSIE *begins to pick up the feathers from the ground*). Pahson better come on, too. I seed Gussie dis mawnin' and she say she li'ble to call on you tonight. She 'low her time 'bout come.

GINSIE. Humph! Gussie's slow as 'lasses in de winter time. She ain't never birfed a young'un quick.

GERANIUM. She 'low dis'n gwine be soon, do'. She been choppin' cotton right along. Say ain't nair one o' her boys holp 'er chop nair row in de whole field.

GINSIE. Tain't none o' Gussie's chillun no-'count.

GERANIUM (*sitting on the wash tub bench*). Dat's what she say. Say dey lazy jes' lak dey pappy. Say she sho' glad she ain't *marry* dey pappy.

GINSIE (*rising*). Humph! Gussie's skeerd o' work her own self, jes' lak she skeerd o' pains. (*Contemptuously.*) Skeerd! (*Facing* GERANIUM, *a few feathers held tight in the fold of her apron.*) Look at all de folks walkin' 'bout on de earf. Look at all de chilluns litterin' up folks's yards. And den dere's de graveyards. How you think all dem peoples got here? De Lawd ain't handed 'em down on no silver waiter. Dey Ma's birfed 'em, dat's how dey come.

GERANIUM. Eve never had no mammy, Aunt Ginsie.

GINSIE (*clutching the feathers in her apron with one hand and scratching her head with the other*). Dat's so. (*Slowly.*) Dat's right. Eve never had no mammy. (*Suddenly.*) But look how Eve turnt out! (*Pausing.*) And Adam— (*Chuckling.*) Lawd, I allus said ifn twas men dat birfed chillun, dey'd hafter be put to sleep. Adam's done proved hit. (*Chuckling again.*) And Geranium, (*Her face lighting up.*) God was de fus' midwife. He seed Adam thoo wid Eve. Lawd, I *is* got a high callin'. But I ain't studyin' no midwifin' tonight. (*Her face aglow as she raises her eyes heavenward.*) Hit's de *second* bawnin' I'se studyin' 'bout. Jake gwine be bawn agin lak Jesus say. Here, (*Emptying her feathers in* GERANIUM's *apron.*) you take dese fedders, Geranium. (*She opens the shutter a little and calls inside.*) *You* Jake, you hurry up wid dat shavin'!

GERANIUM (*whining, her feet dragging, carelessly shaking out the feathers at the right, so that the yard is once more littered.*) When you gwine let Nazarene come home, Aunt Ginsie?

GINSIE (*taking a brush-broom from beside the doorway and beginning to sweep the yard lightly while* GERANIUM *returns to the doorstep*). When you larns to behave yo'self and gits to be some 'count. I done promise Viney, and I gwine keep you; but I ain't havin' you put no notions in *my* gal's head.

GERANIUM (*saucily, seating herself on the steps*). Nazarene lak Sam same as I lak Aleck.

GINSIE (*proudly*). Who? My Nazarene? (*Chuckling at the absurdity of the idea.*) Nazarene ain't studyin' no field nigger. Nazarene larnin' how to be a fine housemaid and wait on folks at parties. (*Pausing before the doorway.*) Miss Mary read me a letter fum her gal in Bummin'ham direckly atter Nazarene left here. (*Sweeping toward* GERANIUM.) Lawd when de work piles high, seem lak I cayn't git along widout dat gal, nuther. (*Sweeping before the steps,* GERANIUM'S *feet included.*) Here, you take dis broom and bresh 'roun' dese do' steps yo'self. You is so lazy I fergits you is got hands and feets! (GERANIUM *rises languidly, takes broom, and begins to sweep toward clothesline.*)

GINSIE. Don't you go raisin' no dust on dem clothes! You sweep t'other way. And you git a move on you. (GINSIE *goes over to* JAKE'S *shirt hanging on the line and touches one of the sleeves.*) Ain't a wrinkle in it! Lawd, I sho' done-up Jake's shirt purty dis time. I tuck much pains wid dis babtizin' shirt as I tuck wid de white bishop's robe when he come last Easter. (*Turning to* GERANIUM *and holding out her flattened palms.*) See dese hands, Geranium? Dey b'longs to de best wash-woman in Tuscaloosa County. Dat's what de folks 'roun' here'll tell you! Dese hands is washed de choir robes, and dey is done up de altar cloths fer Miss Mary's church. Dey washes clean, Geranium. (*Dropping her hands and gazing at her cabin.*) I'se aimin' to keep a *clean house,* too. (*Quickly, crossing left to* GERANIUM.) Dat means I ain't havin' no triflin' womens in my house! I'se 'bout to git Jake straightened out, and I'se aimin' to wring sin outen *yo'* heart—same as I wrung dirt outen dem clothes yonder (*pointing to the clothesline*). (*She starts up the steps, knocking over the hair-tonic.*) Look-a-here, Geranium, whar you been a-gittin' dis stuff? And whar you git dat Hoyt's cologne you been a-smellin' up my house wid?

GERANIUM (*a little fearfully*). Aleck brung hit to me, Aunt Ginsie.

GINSIE. Dat yaller Aleck ain't courtin' no gal fer no good. (*Contemptuously.*) A-slippin' up to my house when I'se gone, and a-hidin' out in de ravine. (*Accusingly.*) And you a-watchin' yo' chances to sneak out wid 'im. (*She whistles.*) Think I ain't heerd dat? I heerd it no longer'n last night, too!

GERANIUM (*aggrieved*). I ain't met Aleck last night, Aunt Ginsie.

GINSIE (*picking up the cans under the left window and placing them on the shelf*). Naw, you ain't met 'im last night 'cause you knowed I wa'n't 'sleep and I'd hear you ifn you crept out de bed. Ravines ain't no place to meet a man, Geranium. (*As* GERANIUM *rests her broom against corner of house and indolently lifts several plants to the shelf opposite the one* GINSIE *is arranging.*) I done told Jake when he moved us to de edge o' dis here 'un, dat woods ain't no place to bring up gals.

GERANIUM. Dey *is* full o' snakes.

GINSIE. And sarpints is de enemy o' folks now, same as fer Adam and Eve. And all dem vines and bushes ain't safe, Geranium. Eve done found *dat* out! (*Pondering.*) Looks lak bushes tempts women, same as Eve. (*After*

surveying her plants with satisfaction she looks down at the steps, uncorks the bottle, smells the hair-tonic, and turns toward GERANIUM.) You is gwine bus' dis bottle in de ravine, same as I bus' dat cologne bottle, Geranium. I'd 'bout got Jake offen dem biggest sprees till you started bringing *yo'* smelly stuff in my house. I ain't aimin' to have 'im finish up *dis* bottle lak he finish up my flo' varnish.
(JAKE, *a tall, supple Negro, dressed in light gray trousers, brown shoes newly-shined, and a fresh white undershirt, opens the cabin door. Even after many years of marriage to* GINSIE, *his irresponsible, fun-loving nature is unrestrained. His deep voice is suave. Cunning, rather than laziness, prompts him to gain his ends by pursuing the line of least resistance.*)

JAKE (*standing in the doorway*). Whar my white shirt, Ginsie?

GERANIUM (*running to the clothesline*). I'll git hit, Unker Jake.
(JAKE *steps outside and* GINSIE *stands by cabin door.* GERANIUM *lifts the clothespins from the shirt and it falls from the line into the tub of water.*)

GINSIE. Dere now, see what you done done! How-come you didn't empty dem wash tubs on de hydrangies lak I told you? (*As she wrings out the shirt.*) You is too lazy, dat's why.
(*Unobserved by* GINSIE *and* GERANIUM, JAKE *has picked up the "anti-kink," examined the label, and uncorked the bottle. Having held the bottle to his nose, he stows it in a back pocket of his trousers with a sigh of satisfaction.*)

JAKE (*starting off*). Nemmine, Ginsie, I guess I kin step down town and run across somebody wid a white shirt on.

GINSIE (*the shirt in her hands as she blocks his exit*). You ain't goin' nowheres.

JAKE. Aw now, honey, tain't no harm to run out and borry fer a me*more*able 'casion lak dis here 'un.

GINSIE (*with finality*). All my fambly ever had to borry was grace fum de Lawd. (*Looking straight at him.*) And you sho' got to ax Him fer a plenty o' *dat*, ifn *you* sees de Kingdom!

JAKE (*taking the shirt from her*). Hand me dat shirt. (*Placatingly, as she glares at him.*) I'll git Frank to iron hit, Ginsie. He done a right good job o' dese pants, yistiddy. (*Carefully concealing the bulge in his back pocket, he turns slowly, examining the creases in his trousers.*)

GINSIE (*studying the trousers*). Frank do iron purty good, ifn he ain't nothin' but a butler. (*Proudly.*) But Miss Mary ain't turned over her table linens to 'im, she ain't.

JAKE. Frank got a 'lectic iron, do', and dat irons quick.

GINSIE (*as* JAKE *starts off right*). Don't you and Frank scorch dat shirt! (*She follows him and stands watching him go.*) Lawd, ifn, his *soul* ain't scorched, I dunno de reason why! (*She turns and going toward the cabin with a sigh, she picks up* GERANIUM's *small mirror*). Look a-here, gal, what you done wid dat hair-tonic? (GERANIUM *remains silent.*) Is you bus' dat bottle lak I told you?

GERANIUM (*fearfully*). Nawm. Unker Jake, he come outen de house jes' atter you say bus' de bottle, and den de shirt hit... hit fell in de water and...

GINSIE (*shaking her*). You mouthin' good-fer-nothin'!

GERANIUM. I fergot, Aunt Ginsie! (*As* GINSIE *continues to shake her.*) I'se... so sor-ry! I'll... go see... ifn Unker... Jake... tuck hit....

GINSIE (*hurling* GERANIUM *across the yard*). Hit takes a 'sperienced 'oman to handle mens lak Jake! (*Flinging the mirror into the flower bed.*) I'll fotch 'im! (*She marches off, right.*)
(GERANIUM, *her arms hanging limply to her sides, goes to the flower bed, picks up her mirror, gazes at her reflection, and shakes her head in displeasure. Pulling her hair through her fingers in an attempt to straighten it, she goes indoors. Almost immediately she comes out with a bundle of clothing tied in a red-checkered cloth. After glancing cautiously around the yard, she hides the bundle under the steps. Suddenly she hears her name called softly. She listens for a moment and comes down into the yard. From the direction of the ravine a soft voice again calls her name.*)

GERANIUM. Who dat call me?

Voice (*feeble, pleading*). Help me up dis bank, Geranium. (Geranium *goes around the left of the house to the edge of the ravine at the rear.*)

Voice. Oh, Lawd!

Geranium (*peering over the edge of the ravine*). How you git home, Nazarene?

Nazarene (*as* Geranium *pulls her up into the yard*). I runned away and kotch de bus. (*Doubling over, evidently in pain.*) Oh, Jesus, I'se got a load to carry!

Geranium (*as* Nazarene, *a stocky, soot-black girl of about sixteen, wearing a pink dress, gay sandals and socks, a three-quarter-length scarlet coat, and a cheap straw hat trimmed with large bright flowers, stumbles across the yard*). Whar yo' things?—I don't see no load.

Nazarene (*sinking down on the yard seat between the twin oaks*). You'll see hit soon enough....

Geranium. What you done wid yo' things, Nazarene? Whar yo' clothes?

Nazarené (*supporting her aching body as she gasps between pains*). I...I'se a-carryin'...all...I'se...got. (*Relieved momentarily of the spasm of pain, she looks up, pushing her hat on the back of her head. She mops the perspiration from her brow with the back of her hand.*) Whar Sam?

GERANIUM (*indifferently*). I dunno. (*Looking down at* NAZARENE.) Reckon I better go fotch 'im?

NAZARENE (*alarmed*). Naw you don't, Geranium. Naw you don't. He a field nigger and Mammy'll brain 'im. —Oh, Lawd! (*She is seized with another paroxysm of pain, to which she nervously reacts with a giggle.*) Dat bus sho' done shuck me up!

GERANIUM (*glancing down the road and turning back to* NAZARENE). I 'spects you better be gittin' in de house.

NAZARENE (*wringing her hands*). I cayn't!

GERANIUM. De pahson'll be here direckly, Nazarene. (*Chuckling.*) He comin' to babtize yo' pa.

NAZARENE (*giggling, she starts to rise; then wailing, she stares hopelessly at the steps.*) I cayn't clom no steps, Geranium....

GERANIUM (*supporting her and forcing her to rise*). Mebbe you cayn't, but jes' de same you *is*.

NAZARENE (*leaning on* GERANIUM *as she goes slowly toward the cabin*). I'se et a heap o' watermelons, but dis is sho' one dat stayed wid me....

GERANIUM (*stepping back from her*). Is you outen yo' head, Nazarene? Watermelons ain't ripe, yit.

NAZARENE. Dis here 'un is.... (*She sinks wearily on the steps and looks up, a tragic expression in her big, tired*

eyes.) Me and Sam, Geranium, ... we was walkin' home fum prayer meetin'.... We clom de fence ... and stop on de edge o' Jedge Winston's melon patch dat night. Twa'n't no harm—Jedge Winston wouldn't-a keerd—he had a *big* crap last year. And we never ... et ... but dat ... one. (*Drawing in her breath with pain.*) Oh, Lawd, what I done done!
(*There is a whistle from the direction of the ravine— the same signal* GINSIE *heard.*)

GERANIUM (*excitedly*). Dat's Aleck! I'se got my clothes hid under dese steps, Nazarene. Me and Aleck's gwine run away tonight! Aleck say we gwine git married when we gits to Bummin'ham. (*The whistle is repeated.*) You git inside, quick! (*Jerking* NAZARENE *to her feet.*) Aleck done found out Aunt Ginsie's gone. I knows it, caze he whistlin' out bold lak dat. He comin' up here, sho'! (*Opening the door and pushing* NAZARENE *inside.*) Git on in dere. Quick! (GERANIUM *starts toward the ravine, but halts as* NAZARENE *calls from indoors. As* NAZARINE *calls a second time, she turns back.*) Git on in de bed, Nazarene. I'll be dere direckly.

NAZARENE (*opening the left shutter by the bed on which she has flung herself*). Geranium? (*Weakly.*) Geranium! (*Rising on her elbow, her head in the window.*) Don't tell Mammy me and Sam is married, will you? She won't mind 'bout de baby—she laks babies—but, fer Jesus' sake, don't tell 'er I is *married!*

GERANIUM (*assuringly*). I ain't gwine tell 'er. (*Slamming the shutter.*) Now you keep quiet!

GINSIE (*calling off-stage, right, as she comes up panting*). Geranium! Geranium! (*Crossing the yard as GERANIUM reluctantly turns once more from the ravine.*) I better not ketch dat whistlin' jay bird on my primmisies! (*She hears a moaning inside the cabin and halts suddenly.*) What dat noise? (*Turning to GERANIUM.*) Tain't Jake?

GERANIUM (*marking time*). Whar Unker Jake, Aunt Ginsie? Hadn't you better go fotch 'im fer de babtizin'?

GINSIE (*disgusted*). Jake couldn't walk straight to he Sad-dy night bath, let alone to no babtizin'. (*Sighing as she sits down on the wash-bench.*) I got to move de day up agin, Geranium. You go tell de pahson a Sad-dy is too late in de week fer Jake.
(GERANIUM, *obviously relieved, starts off right. A wail comes from inside the cabin.* GINSIE *rises.*)

GINSIE. Wait dere, Geranium. (*Crossing to cabin.*) I'se hearin' curious sounds in dat house.

GERANIUM. Hit's ... hit's Nazarene, Aunt Ginsie. (*Nervously.*) She ... she come home to see you.... She takin' a little rest on de bed....

GINSIE (*pushing* GERANIUM *aside and stalking up the steps*). Nazarene! Whar you, chile?
(GERANIUM *goes to the ravine, peers over its edge, and returns to the cabin door.*)

GERANIUM (*calling from the yard*). Does you want me to go git Doctuh Bob, Aunt Ginsie?

GINSIE (*from the open doorway, her hands on her hips*). I ain't needin' no doctuh! Who you think brung all dese chillun clutterin' up folks's houses? Who you think brung *you?*—I brung dis business to dis country, gal—me and de Lawd. (*Pointing to the clotheslines.*) Hand me down one o' dem sheets. (GERANIUM *snatches a sheet from the line as* GINSIE *steps down into the yard.*)

GINSIE. Hit's 'bout time you larned sumpum 'bout dis business, yo' *own* self. Hit mought come in handy some day. Git in dere and tie dis sheet to de bedpost. Here, (*Knotting a corner of the sheet.*) tell 'er to ketch holt o' dis knot and pull hard.

GERANIUM (*shrinking back*). I'se skeerd, Aunt Ginsie!

GINSIE. Dat's what all dis no-'count generation say. (*Derisively.*) Skeerd! Pity Nazarene ain't been skeerd 'fo' now. (*Thrusting the sheet in* GERANIUM'S *reluctant hands.*) Git on in dere! (GERANIUM *goes inside, closing the door behind her.*) Tell 'er de harder she pull, de quicker she'll be. (*Suddenly.*) *Lawdy,* I clean fergot dat pahson! (*Turning back to the cabin and opening the shutter by* GERANIUM'S *bed.*) Dat's hit, knot hit tighter to de bedpost, Geranium. (*Closing the shutter and turning away.*) And me ... me ... de presi*dint* o' de Daughters o' Holiness! (*Suddenly turning to the shutter and peeping inside.*) You hurry up in dere; you know we ain't got no time to waste! (*She closes the shutter, crosses the yard, and peers down the road, her hand shading her eyes.*)

GERANIUM (*from behind closed shutters*). Aunt Ginsie! Come here, Aunt Ginsie!

GINSIE (*calmly as she turns toward the cabin*). I knows my business.

GERANIUM (*in the doorway*). Nazarene say she want *you*, Aunt Ginsie. She say she need you!

GINSIE (*still calm*). Git on back in dere, gal. I knows what I'se doin'. (*She moves up to the doorway.*) Make 'er mad, Geranium. Make lak I don't kere nothin' 'bout 'er. De madder she git, de quicker she'll be.

GERANIUM. You want me to go git some folks to laugh at 'er lak you calls in de neighbors to hurry up Gussie's babies?

GINSIE (*going down to stage–right again*). I cayn't ax nobody to *dis* bawnin'.
(GERANIUM *goes inside, closing the door after her.* GINSIE *walks to the edge of the yard and looks off down the road.*)

GERANIUM (*rushing out, her eyes rolling*). She need sumpum more'n a bedpost, Aunt Ginsie! She ... she ... good and mad!

GINSIE (*hurrying to the house*). Clear out o' my way, gal!
(ALECK, *a slim, loose-jointed mulatto wearing a dark coat with a full-blown red rose in its lapel, white duck trousers, and white "easy-walkers," peers around the left side of the house.*)

ALECK (*softly*). Geranium!

GERANIUM (*startled, and then whispering loudly as she sees* ALECK). Git on 'way fum here, Aleck! (ALECK *backs away and* GERANIUM *goes to the side yard at the left.*)

ALECK (*cautiously approaching her*). Ever'thing's set fer de weddin', Geranium. (GERANIUM *digs her toe in the ground and giggles.* ALECK, *growing bolder, tries to draw her to him.*)

GERANIUM. Go 'way fum here, Aleck. (*Pulling back.*) Ifn Aunt Ginsie know you hangin' 'roun', I cayn't never slip off tonight.

ALECK (*producing two bus tickets*). Come on *now*, den. Let's go ketch de five o'clock bus. (*Holding the tickets before* GERANIUM'S *eyes.*) Dese here reads "Bummin'-ham," Geranium! Does you hear dat, honey?
(*From inside the cabin comes the sound of a child being spanked and the unmistakable cry of a newborn baby.* ALECK *and* GERANIUM *listen, wondering.*)

ALECK. What dat noise, Geranium? (*He takes a step toward the cabin and turns to* GERANIUM *as the cabin grows strangely still.*) Look-a-here, (*Thrusting the bus tickets in his pocket.*) what's been goin' on 'roun' dis place, anyhow?

GERANIUM. Tain't nothin'. Aunt Ginsie's got comp'ny, dat's all.

ALECK (*doubtfully*). Her comp'ny sho' visits *young*. (*He laughs in amusement.*) Is womens done tuck to comin' to Miss Ginsie's *house* when dey wants 'er to see 'em thoo?

GERANIUM (*forgetting her embarrassment in her relief of* ALECK's *solution of the mystery*). Yeh, dat's hit! (*As if to dismiss the discussion.*) Aunt Ginsie ain't got no time to go trapesin' all over de country ever' time somebody birfs a young'un.

ALECK. I reckon you is right 'bout dat. Miss Ginsie sho' is pop'lar. But look-a-here, honey, while Miss Ginsie's got 'er mind on 'er business, let's us go make dat nex' bus!

GERANIUM. I cayn't run off nowhere till atter de pahson come to babtize Unker Jake, Aleck. Aunt Ginsie'll be out here direckly and she'd come a-lookin' fer us. I dunno 'bout you, but she kin allus find me.

ALECK (*sighing*). I reckon we'll hafter wait on de sebem o'clock bus, den. (*Suddenly turning to her.*) But tain't no reason why we cayn't walk down to de spring, is dere? (*Trying to draw her toward the ravine.*) Come on, sweet cakes. Let's go set by de spring whar we kin talk. Miss Ginsie ain't comin' atter no water dis time o' day.

GERANIUM (*wrenching away from him*). I cayn't, Aleck. (*Nervously glancing toward the house.*) Aunt Ginsie, she ... she mought need me.

ALECK. Aw, come on, sugar. I got a s'prise fer you.

GERANIUM (*beaming with anticipation as she turns to him from where she stands*). Whut, Aleck?

ALECK (*trying to appear casual*). Jes' a sort o' little weddin' supper, honey. I seed a truck come in fum Floridy dis mawnin'—(*Betraying his enthusiasm*)—a truck full o' de biggest, juciest, watermelons ever was growed! (*His mouth watering as he continues to stretch his hands wider and wider apart while exaggerating the size of the melons.*) Umn ... umph!

GERANIUM. A *watermelon*, did you say?

ALECK. I sho' did. I hid it in de creek jes' below de spring. Umph, but hit's *good* and ripe. Hit oughter be good and cold now, too!
(GERANIUM *has slowly backed away from* ALECK, *her eyes narrowing. She starts to run around to the back of the house, but* ALECK *seizes her by the wrist and draws her back into the front yard.*)

GERANIUM (giving ALECK *a sound pop on the jaw as she struggles free*). Don't you say watermelon to *me*!
(*Both are suddenly motionless as the door of the cabin opens.* ALECK *disappears in the ravine at left, and* GERANIUM *affects innocence.*)

GINSIE (*a blanket in her arms, descending toward* GERANIUM). Come 'ere, Geranium. Jes' look a-here, will you? (*Turning back a fold of the blanket.*) I'se brung white babies, and I'se brung all de shades o' black babies, but dis here boy is de finest ever I seed! Doctuh Bob couldn't a-done no better! (GERANIUM *peers down at the baby.*) Looks lak my gran'chillun's gwine out-do my chillun, don't hit?

GERANIUM (*suddenly glancing up, looking down the road at the right. She nudges* GINSIE). Here comes de pahson, Aunt Ginsie!
(*The* PARSON, *a tall, deliberate man of sixty-five, wearing sleazy black trousers, a heavy black Prince Albert coat, a stiff-bosomed white shirt with high celluloid collar, narrow black bow-tie, and a sanctimonious air, advances with long, measured strides, a large bouquet wrapped in newspaper in his hand.*)

PARSON. Well, Sis Ginsie, de joyful 'casion is come at last. I rejoices wid you! (*Turning to* GERANIUM.) Ev'nin', Miss Macknolia.

GERANIUM (*shyly*). Ev'nin', Pahson.

PARSON. De sistren and de bredren rejoices wid you, too, Sis Ginsie. Dey rejoices in de sanctity o' yo' home. You is long been sanctified, sister. And whar dere's good, hit's bound to spread. Sich a example as yourn is got to shed light in de end.
(*During the* PARSON'S *speech,* GINSIE *makes several attempts to hand the baby to* GERANIUM; *but* GERANIUM, *intent on removing her apron and tossing it around the corner of the house without attracting the attention of the* PARSON, *fails to notice* GINSIE'S *signals.*)

PARSON. De Daughters o' Holiness sends you dis token o' dey regard, Sis Ginsie. (*He extends the collection of bright flowers, their stems still wrapped in newspaper.*)

GINSIE. Take de *bow*-kay, Geranium. (GERANIUM *takes the bouquet.*) Go put de flowers in some water. (*Sharply, as* GERANIUM *starts up the steps.*) Take 'em 'roun' de back way, gal.

PARSON (*As* GERANIUM *goes*). Dey is fer yo' own holy house, sister—fer yo' table whut is allus set so bountiful.

GINSIE (*curtsying*). Thanky, Pahson.

PARSON. And now, whar de sinner whut's come to 'pentance, sister?

GINSIE (*anxiously, as she turns toward the cabin door*). Jes' lemme put dese blankets in de house, Pahson.

PARSON. Sho', sister, sho'. You done right to sun yo' beddin' on a bright day lak dis here 'un. My wife toted her mattress out dis mawnin' 'bout sun-up. (JAKE *reels in from the rear of the yard. As he rounds the right corner of the house he staggers forward, bumping into* GINSIE.)

JAKE. 'Scuse me, honey.... (*Holding out the shirt, now soiled and limp.*) Here de shirt.... I couldn't find Frank.... (*Laughing loudly as he turns to the* PARSON.) Guess you don't mind waitin' till I gits my shirt on, Pahson? (*The* PARSON, *though astonished at* JAKE's *undignified appearance, nods consent.* JAKE, *starting toward the door, stops suddenly as the baby wails. The* PARSON's *disapproval of him, as well as* GINSIE's *malicious eyes, are lost to him as he gazes in amazement at the partially uncovered face of the baby in the "bedding" he has disarranged.*)

JAKE. Whut dis, honey? Law, 'oman, you sho' works fast! (*Turning to the* PARSON.) I knowed she was smart, Pahson, but I never knowed she was dis smart! (*Looking at* GINSIE, *he waves his shirt in the air.*) Now we *is* gwine celebrate! (*Gazing down at the baby.*) Now ain't dat rascal de spittin' image o' *me?*

GINSIE (*regaining her composure and crossing down left to the* PARSON). Hit's de baby we wants babtized today, Pahson.

JAKE (*realizing his one chance of escape*). I reckon I better step down town and git de baby a little present—bein' dis he birfday. (*As he moves off, he watches* GINSIE *from the corner of his eye.*)

GINSIE (*obviously relieved*). Dat's right, Jake, you run 'long 'fo' de stores shet up.
(*The* PARSON *looks away and* GINSIE *gives* JAKE *a menacing look, jerking her head toward the road she means him to follow without delay. She turns toward the* PARSON *as* JAKE *staggers off right.*)

GINSIE. And now, Pahson, go in and enjoy a little *repast* I fixed fer you. (*To* GERANIUM *who has returned from around the house.*) Geranium, take de Pahson 'roun' to de back o' de house and sarve 'im bountiful. I'se got a little mo' business to tend to inside, (*Nodding toward the closed shutter by* NAZARENE'S *bed.*) 'fo' I jines you-all. (*Apologetically, to the* PARSON.) Not meanin' no disrespec' to yo' pusson, Pahson. Hit's cooler 'roun' de back.

PARSON (*smiling in anticipation*). You don't need to offer no 'pologies, sister. I knows what end o' de house de victuals is ginrally kept. (*He starts to follow* GERANIUM *around the right corner of the cabin but turns back.*) Let's see, do', Sis Ginsie—(*Taking a leather-bound book from his pocket.*) I 'spects we better git dis business straight 'fo' we starts de feastin' and de ceremony: (GINSIE *walks down the steps and the* PARSON *puts on his spectacles and takes out a pencil.* GERANIUM, *with an air of boredom, sits down on the wash-bench. The* PARSON *adjusts his spectacles and peers over their rims at* GINSIE *who stands opposite him.*)

PARSON. Whut de name o' dis chile?

GINSIE (*studying a moment and then looking up with a happy flash of inspiration*). Well, Pahson, since he gwine be a member o' yo' church, I b'lieves his folks would sorter lak to call 'im atter *you.*

PARSON (*pleased*). A good Bible name, sister. Not no fancy name; but a name de Lawd thought good enough to write down in de Good Book. (*Slowly writing.*) Fus' name, *Dan'l;* middle name, *Amos;* (*Looking up.*) Whut's de *last* name, sister?

GINSIE (*lowering her eyes and then raising them as she begins to see her way out of this difficulty*). Nemmine 'bout de last name, Pahson. (*Recovering her compo-*

sure.) We is Christians. And you know, you say yo'-self, hit's de Christian name dat counts.

PARSON. A-men, sister! We is Christians. And, lak I allus said, hit's de Christian name dat counts.

GERANIUM (*from the wash-bench, swinging her legs*). Den let de white folks go on callin' us by our *fus'* names, den. *We* don't kere.

GINSIE. You talks too much, Geranium. Git on in dat room (*Pointing to the door.*) and stay wid my patient till I calls you. Me and little Amos Dan'l is 'scortin' de Pahson to de feastin' board dis time. (*Raising the baby to her shoulder and patting it with pride,* GINSIE *marches around right to the kitchen, followed by the* PARSON. GERANIUM, *pouting, goes toward the front room of the cabin.*)

NAZARENE (*opening the shutter by her bed and peering out*). Geranium, ain't I never gwine git nothin' t'eat? De smell o' dem victuals is settin' me wild!

GERANIUM (*sullenly*). Seems lak you done et a plenty. (GERANIUM *slowly mounts the steps and the sound of* GINSIE's *cheerful voice can be heard above the pleasant rattle of dishes and spoons in the kitchen where the* PARSON *is being served.*)

GINSIE (*calling from the supper table*). You Geranium! You come 'ere and take dis plate to de patient.

GERANIUM (*pausing on the last step to gaze through the window at* NAZARENE *who has sunk back on her pillow with the promise of food*). Mo' watermelon, I reckon!

WATERMELON TIME

The Parson (*about to baptize the baby*). Whut de name o' dis chile?
Ginsie. Nemmine 'bout de last name, Pahson. (*Recovering her composure.*) And you know, you say yo'self, hit's de Christian name dat counts.

(*To* Ginsie, *wearily, as she goes indoors.*) I'se comin', Aunt Ginsie.
(*The door closes behind* Geranium *and there is a whistle from the ravine. The signal is repeated, loud and insistent this time. The door is cracked. Opening it wider,* Geranium, *on her knees, thrusts her head out, peeping around left, and then right. Suddenly she reaches her arm stealthily under the steps, tugs at the bundle of clothing she had hidden there, and draws it up to the top step. She looks all about her but does not see* Aleck *who is cautiously making his way from the ravine at left, a huge slice of watermelon in his hands.* Aleck, *sidling close to the cabin, steals to the left corner of the house and peers around at* Geranium. *She sees him beckon to her. For a moment she wavers, her eyes bulging, her mouth watering, as she gazes longingly at the melon. But, summoning all the strength of her will, she darts backward, snatching her bundle inside.*)

Ginsie (*calling pleasantly from the kitchen*). Geranium! Don't you want no supper, chile?

Geranium (*cheerfully*). I'se comin', Aunt Ginsie!
(*With a quick motion of finality the door is slammed.* Aleck, *having failed to lure* Geranium *from the cabin with the favorite treat of all Black Belt darkies, slinks hopelessly across the yard as the sound of the door-latch indicates to him that* Geranium *has "larnt sumpum." He goes out of the yard to the road, consoling himself by sinking his teeth into the juicy red watermelon.*)

CURTAIN

PARTY DRESS

A PLAY OF THE BACK COUNTRY

Written in the playwriting course at the University of North Carolina and originally produced by the Carolina Playmakers on July 2, 1940.

THE CHARACTERS

JOE BENSON,
   a tenant farmer of southern Alabama   Neil Hartley
MELISSA, *his wife*   Laurraine Goreau
MARTIE, *his sister*   Mollie Holmes

SCENE: The living room of the Benson farmhouse in a remote section of southern Alabama.

TIME: The present. Twilight of an April day.

THE SCENE

The scene is the kitchen-livingroom of the Benson's unpainted farmhouse in the back country of southern Alabama. It is twilight of a balmy April day. A fire, on which supper is cooking, is smoldering in the stone fireplace at the left. In the center of the rear wall, its thick boards running lengthwise, is a door which leads to the dilapidated front porch. On each side of this door is a window of small square panes. None of the openings affords a glimpse of the flowering peach trees or scattered plum- and briar-thickets dotting the half-tilled, unfenced hillside. Skimpy pink curtains with tie-backs of green crepe-paper almost conceal the vari-colored geraniums and begonias in tin cans and broken granite vessels of many shapes and sizes, arrayed on crude shelves flanking the edge of the porch. Near the right window is a square oak table covered with a starched white cloth. It bears a kerosine-lamp of glass adorned with a home-made shade of green crepe-paper, and a jelly glass filled with sprays of blackberry bloom. To the left of the table, against the rear wall, is a book-case made of stacked wooden boxes brought, along with sundry purchases, from various trips to the country store. A battered old walnut cupboard stands in the left corner, between the fireplace and the left window. It contains dishes, cutlery, a meagre supply of groceries, and sundry household articles. On the top of the cupboard is a thick glass of trailing white plum branches. To the left of the front door is a home-made table on which rests a cedar water-bucket with gourd dipper, a dented wash-pan, and a soap tray. Above the stand is a shelf on which lie a blue celluloid comb and a matching brush. A small mirror hangs just above the shelf and there is a fresh roller-towel close by. On the unpainted walls are three large picture calendars of former years. On the mantel are a clock in an old wooden frame, a box of matches, and a medicine bottle. To the left of the fireplace, down-stage, is a wood-box containing several hickory logs and a piece of wood suitable for whittling. A few straight chairs with cane seats and a low, matching rocker, are scattered about the room. At right-center is an oblong table of unpainted pine which supports one end of an ironing board; the other end rests on the back of a chair. In the right wall opposite the fireplace is a door opening into a bedroom.

MARTIE BENSON, *a fair slender girl of seventeen, stands behind the ironing board pressing the last organdie flounce of her white "party dress." Her feet are bare and she is clad in faded blue calico. Her sensitive face is flushed and eager as she turns the ruffled skirt on the padded board. There is grace and deftness in each swift movement of her capable hands, and in her lithe figure. Her light-brown hair, falling in natural waves to her shoulders, lends an added softness to her delicate beauty.*

JOE BENSON, *several years* MARTIE'S *senior, sits beside the fire slowly plying the wooden dasher of an old earthen-ware churn. He is a sturdy masculine likeness of his sister, his bushy brown hair carelessly pushed back from his broad forehead and fine gray eyes. But he is awkward and loose-limbed and his hands, like his face, are hardened and reddened by toil in sun and wind. He has come in from a day of plowing and, clad in blue denim overalls and frayed shirt, now sits with sleeves rolled up, collar unfastened, and red earth still clinging to his shoes. The large brown churn rests on the hearth between his sprawled knees as he moves the dasher cheerfully but lazily, glancing from time to time at* MARTIE, *and occasionally lifting the top of the churn to peer inside.*

MARTIE (*raising the end of the ironing-board resting on the chair and cautiously removing the dress before turning to* JOE, *the white yoke against her bare white throat, the skirt carefully guarded from the floor*). There! I guess that looks good enough to wear to any dance. (*Proudly.*) You wouldn't know I'd worn it to everything in Shady Grove for the past two years. Now, would you, Joe?

JOE (*stopping the churn-dasher as* MARTIE *walks toward him, the white waist pressed against her high breasts, cascades of ruffling held in a manner to conceal her old blue calico*). Sure wouldn't, Sis. (*Slowly.*) I reckon you're like Ma, though. You-all always could make sumpum out o' nothin'.

MARTIE (*laughing a little and regarding the dress with satisfaction*). Not quite, Joe. A woman's got to have a scrap o' somethin' to start with.

JOE (*turning his chair toward* MARTIE *as he watches her fluff the skirt*). Thought you were goin' to flute the ruffles like Ma always fluted yo' Sunday dresses. Didn't Lissie tell you I fixed Ma's old flutin' irons for you?

MARTIE (*draping the dress over a chair beside the small oak table and rearranging the flounces*). Yes, Liss told me. But I'm savin' the flutin' for Easter. Miss Nettie Holoman's goin' to give me a blue ribbon sash if I help her get ready for her kinfolks that's comin' to the revival. (*Glancing back at the dress, she goes back to the ironing-board.*) With a blue silk sash, it'll seem almost like a new dress. (JOE *begins churning again and she picks up the iron, starts toward the hearth, but stops to gaze at the foamy mass of organdie.*) And the *next* spring, I'm goin' to dye it pink!

JOE (*turning farther around to look at the window as* MARTIE *kneels on the hearth*). With red ink, like you done them winder curtains, I reckon.

MARTIE (*turning from the fire on which she has placed the iron*). They don't look so bad to be made out of flour sacks, do they? (*Proudly she steps forward to survey first one window and then the other.*) Sym Keeler gave me the crepe paper. It was left over from decoratin' the store for the dance. (*Gaily, as she stands the ironing-board in the far corner by the cupboard and comes down to the table.*) But it took the whole bottle of ink to dye those flour sacks, Joe. You'll have to buy me another bottle before I can dye my dress next spring.

JOE (*chuckling*). Maybe Hamp Walker will get in some for his new store. Reckon I won't have to buy none, then.

MARTIE (*saucily*). I'm not carin' what Hamp Walker puts in his store.

JOE (*as* MARTIE *takes a match from the mantel and lights the lamp*). Hamp's got a right nice place, Martie. Too far out in the woods for trade, maybe. But it sure is handy, hitched on to the front o' his house like that. And there's bound to be some passin' at the Cross Roads some time. It looks right pretty, too. Tain't painted, nor fancy, nor nothin' like that. But the boards are all new and clean. And it helps to hide that ol' shack Hamp's been a-bachin' in.

MARTIE (*throwing the burned-out match in the fire*). It's time Hamp Walker put up *somethin'* to hide that old shack—even if he is a-bachin'.

JOE (*drily*). Well, I ain't a-sayin' he's always goin' on a-bachin'. (*With a roguish glance at* MARTIE.) And I reckon he ain't exactly give you that notion, either.

MARTIE (*tensely*). Oh, Joe, hush!

JOE (*in surprise*). What's the matter? You and Hamp ain't fell out, have you? Ain't he comin' by to take you to the dance, tonight?

MARTIE (*arranging the chair*). Not this time. He ... He always ... always ...

JOE (*suspicious*). Always what?

MARTIE (*both hands clenched on the back of the chair at the right of the pine dining-table, turns to* JOE). Oh, Joe, he ... he always calls me ... Mattie! And I can't stand it! Not when I'm dressed up, I can't!

JOE (*pushing the churn aside*). Well I'll swan. Of all the dern, womanish reasons.

MARTIE. Oh, I know it sounds silly to you! But when he calls me "Mattie," I *am* Mattie—just plain Mattie—'cause I'm with him! (*On the verge of angry tears.*) And that's the way he wants me. Even when I'm dressed up, and lookin' like somebody, he makes me remember I'm not.

JOE (*gently*). But you are somebody, Martie. You know Ma always said—

MARTIE. Yes, Ma believed in us. And if she'd lived, she'd have seen that we amounted to somethin' (*Slowly.*) But we haven't turned out like she meant us to, Joe.

JOE (*thoughtfully, as* MARTIE *goes to window at right and stares outside*). I reckon you're right, Martie. (*After a pause, as he watches her.*) But it's my fault if you ain't had things like Ma planned 'em.

MARTIE (*going quickly to him*). No it's not, Joe. I shouldn't have talked like that. (*Standing behind him, she strokes his hair.*) You've got Lissie and the children now and you couldn't do any more than you're doin'. And it's not your place to look after a grown-up girl like me. (*Her voice unsteady as she nods toward the dress she has ironed and forces a little laugh.*) Why, I let down the last tuck of my white dress last Easter. (JOE *is silent, deeply moved; he raises his hand to clasp her own.*) Why don't you and Lissie go to the dance, tonight? It would make you and her ... feel better.

JOE (*smiling as he gazes down at his mud-covered shoes which he stretches out before him*). I reckon these ol' muddy clod-hoppers are better fit for the field than Sym Keeler's fresh-scrubbed dance floor.

MARTIE (*enthusiastically*). You can clean 'em in no time, Joe! And I ironed your good shirt this mornin'.

JOE (*yawning*). Nope. A married man's feet have got another kind o' steppin' to do. (*Teasing.*) Anyhow, I might go callin' some girl by the wrong name.

MARTIE (*seriously*). Somebody called me "Martha" once, Joe.

JOE (*as* MARTIE *goes toward the wash-stand.*) Well, that's what Ma named you, ain't it?

MARTIE (*turning from the shelf as she picks up her brush after primping her hair in the mirror*). Yes, but he . . . he didn't know that, Joe. He said . . . said I looked like a girl named Martha in an opera called that.

JOE (*puzzled*). A opery?

MARTIE (*sitting on the floor beside his chair*). Yes, an opera. That's a long, pretty story written in songs . . . with lots of other music. (*She begins to brush her hair, speaking slowly, forgetting for a time* JOE's *presence and re-living the ecstasy of her dream of first love.*) We were walkin' home from the dance and we could still hear the music. I was wearin' my white dress and it looked all silver in the moonlight—like he said the rose in my hair looked. (*Unconsciously touching her hair with the tips of her fingers.*) He stopped just before we got to the white cherry on the edge of the pasture, and he said ... said "Wait, and let me look at you. Why, you're just like the girl in the opera! No wonder your name is Martha!" Then he showed me how to fix (*Correcting herself.*) arrange ... flowers ... becomin'. (*Looking up.*) I can smell the cherry blooms now, same as when he broke 'em and fastened 'em on my dress. (*Smiling over her memory, she turns from* JOE *and begins once more slowly to brush her hair.*) And we sat down on the meadow grass and he told me all about the opera. Then he sang some tunes and I ... I felt ... (*Suddenly remembering* JOE *and adding quickly as she rises.*) like the girl in the opera, I reckon. (*She walks away and then turns suddenly to him.*) Joe, do you suppose Sym Keeler told the fiddlers to learn some waltz-pieces like I asked him?

JOE. *Waltz*-pieces?

MARTIE (*laying her brush on the shelf.*) Yes. We're round-dancin', tonight. Larry ... Mr.—I mean the young man that walked home with me from the dance that night— Well, he ... (*Excitedly.*) he taught me! See— (*Waltzing slowly.*) It goes like this!

JOE (*rising and standing with his back to the fire.* MARTIE *begins to count "one-two-three, one-two-three," etc., while dancing*). Tain't pretty as the square-dance figgers. Tain't nothin' to it, as I can see.

MARTIE. Oh, but there is, Joe. Come here and I'll show you! (*She pushes the pine table farther down front and moves the straight chair out of her way.*) Put your arm around me, Joe. (*Showing him the position.*) This way. Now, I'll lead this time. (*She begins to hum "The Missouri Waltz," and* JOE *awkwardly attempts to follow her steps.*) No! (*Stopping suddenly.*) You must start off on the other foot. There. (*They make a better beginning.*) That's better. That's right, Joe! (*Humming the same tune.*) Keep time, now. (*She resumes the chorus as they circle about the room,* JOE *awkward, but managing to keep in step.*)

JOE. What you keep watchin' that window, for?

MARTIE (*embarrassed, as she turns from window*). Oh, I...I don't know, Joe. I guess there *won't* be anybody comin' this early. (*Falling into position with him.*) Come on, now. I'll pay attention.

JOE (*watching his feet,* MARTIE *starts to waltz him about the room again*). But where we goin', now? How does it wind up? When you change partners?

MARTIE (*dropping* JOE's *hand and moving back from him a little as they stop dancing*). Oh, you don't ever change. That's what's so *nice* about it. Two people keep time together—with the music—and it's all...all ...together...*you* know...like the way a poem goes.

JOE (*doubtfully*). I reckon it'd be all right so long as you started off with the right partner. But Lissie, now, she —I reckon me and her—she'd think it was sort o' foolish, doin' the same thing over and over.

MARTIE (*as* JOE *stands mopping his brow with his cheap colored handkerchief*). Oh, Joe, please! (*Hurrying to the cupboard and taking from it a flannel cloth.*) You and Lissie come to the dance, tonight! (*Pushing* JOE *into his chair by the churn and kneeling to clean his shoes.*) It's always fun at the big spring gatherin'! You used to never miss it. And you know you always had more fun than anybody. (*Thoughtfully.*) Maybe it would make Lissie . . . make her . . . happier.

JOE (*taking the cloth from her*). A farmer's feet don't b'long in no dance hall, Martie. They got to shuffle in the field. (*Looking at her curiously.*) But you're powerful excited 'bout this spring festival. Got a new feller to show off them new steps to?

MARTIE (*going to the mirror*). You wait and see.
(JOE *leans to clean his shoes as* MELISSA, *a thin, sallow woman with weak, drooping mouth, dark, frowning eyes, and stringy, lustreless hair drawn in a tight knot on top of her head, appears in the bedroom doorway. Unseen by* JOE *and* MARTIE, *she watches them sullenly for several moments, a basket of rough-dried clothing clutched under one arm.*)

MELISSA (*eyeing* JOE *and* MARTIE *with disgust as, with a swish of her sagging brown calico skirt, she walks heavily across the floor and dumps the basket on the table*). You kin jes' bring out that ironin' board you put up so quick and finish up these clothes, Martie.

MARTIE (*surprised, turning from primping her hair*). But Lissie . . . You know I've been tellin' you about the spring gatherin' all week. I finished up the whole week's washin' and ironin' this mornin'. I've been rushin' all day so you wouldn't need me, tonight.

JOE (*tossing the cloth onto the hearth as* MELISSA *empties the clothes on the table and places the basket beneath.*) Ever'body's goin' to the spring gatherin', Lissie—all the young folks, anyhow.

MELISSA. Ain't nobody said they wa'n't. (*With a glance at the clock.*) But Martie's got plenty o' time to finish up her work 'fore she goes.

JOE (*gently, as* MARTIE *slowly takes the ironing board from against the wall and places it, as before, across the edge of the pine table and the back of a chair*). But this is Sad-dy night, Lissie. Martie was a-pressin' her party dress, but—you-all don't never iron on Sad-dy night, in general, do you?

MELISSA (*dipping water from the cedar bucket with the gourd and pouring it into the wash-basin while* MARTIE *takes an iron from the fire*). Well, don't folks never git dirty on Sad-dys, I'd like to know? I been a-washin' all ev'nin'—when I wa'n't tendin' to them sick young 'uns! (*Coming down to the table with the basin.*) As if Nancy Bell ain't been a-whoopin' and a-wastin' her victuals all over the flo' fer a month! And now Joey's set in.

JOE (*as* MELISSA *begins to sprinkle the rough-dried clothing she has piled on the table.* MARTIE *places a colored shirt on the ironing board*). But what you want to go wearin' yo'self out with next week's washin' for? You know Martie always has the clothes in the tub early of a Monday.

MELISSA (*pointing to the clothing*). Well, twa'n't Martie that washed them clothes. (*Muttering to herself, she turns back to her sprinkling.*) Off at Nettie Holoman's all ev'nin' a-helpin' 'er clean up fer the preacher.

MARTIE (*glancing at* MELISSA *from time to time as she irons the shirt*). And if I didn't work out sometimes, I'd never have a cent of my own. Never wear anything but your old cast-off, worn-out rags! (*Resting the base of the iron on the board.*) I bunched radishes, countin' em' and tyin' 'em till my fingers bled, to get enough money to pay for that white cloth. (*Pointing to her white dress.*) Two hundred bunches of radishes, counted and tied, for every nickel paid me. (*Her voice almost breaking as she looks down at her hands.*) And the grit and stingin' leaves cuttin' into my hands so I could hardly sew! (*Wheeling on* MELISSA *who never raises her eyes as she sprinkles.*) And you've begrudged me a decent dress ever since I bought it and took time to make it up! (*Ironing furiously, her face bent over the shirt in order to hide her tears.*) Wouldn't even give me a button off the worn-out baby clothes I'd made for little Joey. (*Her voice rising.*) Clothes you wouldn't know how to make!

JOE (*placatingly, as* MARTIE *nervously smooths the shirt*). You see Martie's goin' to do yo' ironin' for you, Lissie. Go and get some rest now, while you can. Me and Martie will fix you some hot supper.

MELISSA (*raising her hand to her head*). A lot o' cookin' Martie's done in the house *this* week! A-wastin' her time a-makin' pink curtains, (*Stepping back from the table to survey the windows and the lamp.*), and paper lamp-shades and all sech foolishness.

JOE. You're wore out, Lissie. Go lie down now, 'fore you work yo'self up into one o' them splittin' headaches.

MELISSA (*hysterically, as she turns toward him*). Ain't no rest, ain't no peace! You a-takin' sides agin me!

JOE (*quietly*). Naw I ain't, Lissie. And I help you all I can in the house.

MELISSA (*raising the dasher to peer inside the churn and quickly slamming dasher and top down in disgust*). You couldn't git a teaspoonful o' butter out o' a greased jersey.

MARTIE (*calmly, as she turns from her ironing*). I'll see about the butter, Lissie. (*Going toward the cupboard and taking from it a crock and a tablespoon.*) Go lie down, now, while the children are quiet. (*She closes the door of the cupboard and looks straight at* MELISSA.) But if you've got anything else you want done tonight, tell me now.

MELISSA (*sarcastically, as she wheels on* MARTIE). You're in somethin' of a swivet to git away, ain't you? Maybe you think you'll see that town feller that larnt you them new steps!

MARTIE (*looking steadily at* MELISSA). Maybe I will. He'd be a welcome sight after the likes o' some folks 'round here.

MELISSA (*as* MARTIE *kneels to lift the dasher from the churn and scrapes the butter into the crock with the spoon*). Different, ain't he? That's what you was a-tellin' 'im the night he brung you home from the spring gatherin' last year. Aw, I heerd yo' pretty talk. And hisn, too. Them moon-flower vines hid you fum me; but I wa'n't sleep like you thought I was, when you and him was a-settin' on the steps out there. (*Pointing toward the front porch.*)

MARTIE (*looking up*). You—you—listened?

MELISSA. What was to keep me fum it? The winder by my bed was up, wa'n't it? (*Sarcastically.*) Asked him to come back, didn't you? Well, maybe the reason he ain't come is 'cause he's different. Maybe he don't like our country ways. Maybe he won't come to the spring gatherin' tonight—no more'n he come to them other dances you been a-rushin' off to.

JOE (*rising from the hearth where he has been tending the food cooking over the slow fire*). Oh, Lissie, that town feller was just somebody passin' through. Martie don't set no store by him.

MELISSA. Ye-es, he was a-passin' through, all right. But it seems Martie ain't fergot *him*. (*Turning to* MARTIE *who has begun to dip the butter from the milk in the churn and add it to the butter in the crock.*) You think

WOOTTEN-MOULTON

PARTY DRESS

MARTIE (*remembering*). I can smell the cherry blooms now, same as when he broke 'em and fastened 'em on my white dress.

I ain't seed you gittin' ready fer ever' dance this year? A-workin' yo'self into a fever like you never done befo', and a-primpin' up the house like the preacher was a-comin'? You think you're goin' to dance with 'im tonight, don't you? (*Stepping forward as* MARTIE *shrinks from her.*) Maybe he'll walk home with you and set out there on the steps agin and tell you he'll take you out o' all this! (MARTIE *lets the spoon slide from her hands and drops her head as* MELISSA's *voice rises louder and more shrill.*) Maybe he'll take you right off from the dance hall, and you won't never have to come back and live with Lissie Hendricks, and have nothin' mo' to do with her folks that ain't equal to yourn!

MARTIE (*rising*). Oh, Liss, hush! It's not that way. You ... you don't understand.

MELISSA. Naw, I don't understand. (*Beginning to move restlessly about the room as* MARTIE *puts the crock of butter and the spoon in the cupboard and* JOE *pulls his chair closer to the fire, bending over to stir a pot of turnips and turn a hoe-cake.*) I'm a Hendricks, and I cayn't understand. (MARTIE *closes the cupboard door and covers the churn.*) Well, 'cause I cayn't read, I cayn't understand them books Joe brung here from his ma's place. (*Pointing to the book-case.*) And I cayn't understand that set o' travel books yo' town beau sent, direckly after you met 'im. (*Taking a step toward* MARTIE.) But I kin understand some things, Martie Benson. Yo' town beau ain't sent you a line o' his own handwritin'. You better be a-listenin' to Hamp Walker

talk, than to be a-waitin' on a mail-carrier with a empty sack!
(*All listen as the sound of a child's cough comes from the bedroom.*)

JOE (*rising*). It's Joey. I'll go this time, Lissie.

MELISSA (*going to the cupboard and taking a teaspoon from a shelf*). Set still, set still. I ain't never seed a man yet what was handy with a sick baby. (*As* MARTIE *takes the medicine bottle from the mantel.*) You're all right to play with 'em, and walk 'em over to the commissary when they're cleaned up (*Striding toward the bedroom.*) but it's me that does the drudgin'.

JOE (*as the child continues to cough*). Lissie, you better let me bring Joey in here to the fire; (*Going toward bedroom.*) it'll quiet 'im.

MELISSA (*turning*). Tain't goin' to be nothin' to quiet when I git through with 'im!

MARTIE (*shaking the medicine bottle*). I'll give Joey his cough medicine, Lissie. (*Anxiously, she steps in front of* MELISSA.) If you scold him, you'll make him cry and he'll cough worse. (*Holding the bottle toward the light.*) Why, it's empty. The medicine's all gone. (*Nervously she runs toward the oak table, places the bottle beside the lamp and snatches up her white dress.*) But I won't let him cry, Lissie. I'll show him and Nancy Bell my pretty dress. (*Excitedly, as* MELISSA *starts to follow her into the bedroom.*) Take the iron off that shirt, Lissie! It's scorchin'! (MARTIE *hurries to the bedroom with the dress, closing the door behind her as* MELISSA *takes the iron from the shirt and stands it endwise on the ironing board.* MELISSA *listens, her head turned toward the bedroom door. Satisfied that there is to be no further disturbance, she draws the rocker toward* JOE'S *chair, its back to the wash-stand, and sits down.)*

MELISSA (*leaning forward*). Hamp Walker was here this ev'nin'.

JOE (*his right foot on the cane seat of his chair, begins to polish his shoe*). Wantin' to see Martie?

MELISSA. Yes, but she was over at Nettie Holoman's.

JOE (*smiling*). Right long walk for Hamp to be takin' for nothin'.

MELISSA. Hamp says Martie ain't been the same since that town feller brung 'er home from the dance that night.

JOE. Oh pshaw, Lissie. That feller was just drivin' through here when his car broke down. You just now said Martie ain't had a line from him since he left here. Why, he was right off soon as Ned Hinson fixed his axle at the blacksmith shop.

MELISSA (*mysteriously*). It takes a right smart piece o' time to fix a bent axle. And you fergit—Ned Hinson's boy was takin' the town feller over to the dance at Sym Keeler's commissary while the axle was bein' fixed. (*With a nod toward the bedroom door.*) And Martie was a-wearin' her white party dress that night.

JOE. Well, tain't no wonder he singled Martie out to dance with. (*Proudly*.) But Martie don't have to dress up to make a feller take notice. (*Standing up straight, both feet on the floor.*) She always could outshine any girl in this beat. Why, she looks good in *yo'* old clothes, Lissie.

MELISSA (*taken back for a moment*). Well, Martie would a-been a sight better off if Ned Hinson's boy had-a left that town feller at the blacksmith shop, stid o' takin' 'im over to the commissary to put notions in the gal's head. Hamp's good as said so, hisself.

JOE (*laughing*). Don't Hamp like them round-dancin' steps the town feller taught Martie? Can't he learn 'em? (*He suddenly remembers his other shoe and rests his left foot on the chair as he begins to clean the mud from it before polishing it.*)

MELISSA. Round-dancin', square-dancin', hit's all the same to Hamp, I reckon. He's lookin' fer a wife to keep his house and run his store while he tends his farm. But he ain't goin' to wait much longer. Cayn't be takin' chances on losin' trade while he's in the field, he says.

JOE (*taking his foot from the chair and dropping the cloth on the upper corner of the hearth*). I reckon it'll be a good while 'fore Hamp builds up much trade. Store too out-o'-the-way. (*Chuckling*.) But I reckon Sym Keeler ain't worryin' 'bout that. (*Pausing as he takes a corn-cob pipe from his pocket.*) Hamp's got a right nice little stock, though. (*As he packs the bowl of his pipe with the rough-cut tobacco he draws from his pocket.*) I was a-tellin' Martie 'bout it last week when I bought the cough syrup for Nancy Bell. (*Lighting the pipe and punctuating his sentence with long puffs.*) Mighty far walk, but I thought I ought to help ol' Hamp out, bein' he was jes' openin' up, and Nancy Bell kep' a-coughin' anyhow. (*He raises his eyes to see* MARTIE *in her white dress, a white rose in her hair, as she comes from the bedroom. She is carrying several magazines on one arm. She pauses for him to admire her dress and he looks at her half proudly, half teasingly.*)

JOE. Martie, since you look so pretty, I reckon you better be the one to walk over to Hamp's for the next bottle o' cough syrup.

MARTIE. Can't I get it at Sym Keeler's commissary, Joe?

JOE. I was just a-teasin' you, Martie. I'll get some medicine, somewhere, if we need it tonight.

MARTIE (*obviously relieved, goes to the square oak table and arranges the magazines beside the lamp before turning to* MELISSA). I'll finish the ironin', Lissie. Nancy Bell wanted me to dress up before she went to sleep.

MELISSA (*going to the table and examining the magazines while* MARTIE *tests the iron on the board, finds it cold, and places it on the fire*). Humph! Style books! Who's got money in this house to spend on clothes?

MARTIE (*quietly, as she kneels on the hearth*). Nobody wants any clothes like the ones in those books, Lissie.

They're just some old household magazines Mrs. Holoman gave me. (*Shyly as she rises and turns toward the table after picking up the iron from the coals.*) I thought they looked kind o' . . . homelike . . . by the lamp there.

JOE (*pleased*). Sure they do. (MARTIE *goes to the board with the hot iron.*) And when we're through with 'em, Nancy Bell can cut out the paper dolls like you used to cut up Ma's old style books, Martie.
(MARTIE *looks up from her ironing to smile at him.* MELISSA *grumbles, turning the pages of the magazines.* JOE *steadies the pot of turnips on the coals. Finding* MARTIE'S *iron in his way, he removes it and places it on the outer corner of the hearth.*)

MELISSA (*fingering the pages*). Always a-clutterin' up the house with some foolishness. Flowers in the middle o' the table where the syrup and the salt and sugar b'longs. Tin cans full o' geraniums a-spillin' dirt on the front porch. And now, weeds! (*Sniffing the glass of blackberry sprays on the table and pushing them farther from her.*) As if twa'n't enough fer berry briars and wild plum thickets to crowd out the fields——let alone a-totin' 'em in the house!

JOE (MELISSA *picks up the medicine bottle on the table and places it on top of the cupboard*). Aw now, Lissie, plum and berry blooms smell sweet in the house—same as outdoors. Nancy Bell likes 'em, too. The front yard's all dug up now with flower peep-shows. I found her a piece o' green glass to put over one just yesterday.

MELISSA (*turning on him*). I reckon it was one of my broke ice-cream saucers. (*She snatches the glass of plum branches from the top of the cupboard, opens the front door, and flings water and flowers outside. JOE and MARTIE watch her as she comes in and closes the door.*)

MELISSA. Them plum branches is too sweet anywheres. (*Going to the cupboard with the glass.*) Anyhow, hit's most suppertime, and I never did like no flower scent mixed up with the smell o' my victuals.

JOE (*remonstrating*). Lissie!

MARTIE. Never mind, Joe, I guess I'll . . . go change . . . my dress, now. (*She goes into the bedroom.*)

JOE (*helplessly*). How you 'spect to eat, Lissie, and you got Martie ironin' on the table?

MELISSA (*going to the fireplace*). Maybe there won't be nothin' fittin' to eat!

JOE. Martie made up the bread after she come from Mrs. Holoman's, Lissie. Everything's right here on the fire. (*Bending over the hearth.*) I sure cooked this hoe-cake pretty and even. Twouldn't hurt these turnips to boil a little longer though.

MELISSA (*going toward the bedroom, her hand pressed to her head*). Well since I got to wait, I'll try to git a little rest. Goodness knows I'm long enough a-gittin' it.

(MELISSA *disappears and* JOE *rises and stands with his back to the fire, his hands clasped behind him, his eyes fixed on the floor. Suddenly he reaches in his pocket and draws out a small package. Pleased with himself, he removes the brown wrapping paper and looks at a small bottle of silver paint and a little brush. After a glance at the bedroom door he hastily wraps his gifts and thrusts the package back into his pocket.*)

JOE (*smiling as* MARTIE *comes toward him in her faded blue calico, the white rose still in her hair*). Cinderella after the ball!

MARTIE (*stopping suddenly as she sees her iron on the corner of the hearth*). Joe Benson! (*Scolding good-naturedly.*) You and your cookin'! You've moved my iron and I'll bet they're both cold.

JOE (MARTIE *picks up the iron she has left on the ironing-board*). Yep, sure are, Mart.

MARTIE (*placing both irons on the fire*). Now we'll have to wait before I can iron. You'll be good and ready for those turnips by the time I clear the table for supper.

JOE (*reaching in his pocket*). Well, while we're waitin', maybe we got time for another little job. (*He walks over to the table and hands* MARTIE *the small package.*)

MARTIE (*tearing the paper wrapping from the bottle of silver paint*). Shoe-gilt! Oh, Joe, I've never worn silver shoes! Where'd you get it?

JOE (*beaming with pride in his gift*). Sym Keeler's commissary. I went by to see how he'd fixed up for the dance and I run across it on the counter. It just come in today, Sym said.

MARTIE (*reading the directions*). It ought to be put on right away.

JOE. It dries quick, Sym said. Take off your shoes and I'll fix 'em for you.

MARTIE (*kicking off her shoes*). Oh, *no*, Joe, *I* want to do it! Let me do *one* shoe, anyway. It'll be fun with this little brush.

JOE. You do the first coat, then. Sym said it would take two coats for black shoes.

MARTIE (*setting the bottle and brush down on the table and quickly removing her white stockings*). I mustn't get these white stockings dirty. They're the only light ones I have. Next year (*Hanging the stockings on the back of a chair.*) I'm goin' to tie more radishes and order silk ones—blue silk ones—to match my blue silk sash!

JOE (*as* MARTIE *pushes the rough-dried clothing aside and begins to paint her shapeless old black slipper*). This is the first time I ever saw a barefooted woman a-workin' with a rose in her hair.

MARTIE (*putting her hand to her hair*). It's from the bride's rose bush we brought from Ma's old place, Joe.

JOE. It'll wilt there. (*Starting to take the rose.*) I'll put it in a cup of water till you get ready to go.

MARTIE (*drawing back*). No, Joe, leave it there.

JOE (*sitting down by the fire and watching* MARTIE). It's a wonder you were willin' to take off yo' pretty dress.

MARTIE (*putting down the shoe and turning to* JOE). You know, Joe, I get a funny feelin' every time I fix up and have to take a nice dress off. (*Beginning to paint again, but pausing from time to time as she turns to* JOE *who has begun to whittle on a small stick from the wood-box*). It's the same way I felt when I was little and Ma was takin' in sewin' after Pa died. You know how Ma always fitted other girls' dresses on me when I was their size. When she'd finish, she slid the dresses down from my neck and over my arms and hands. Sometimes they touched my bare legs and feet. I remember just how the different kinds o' cloth felt. Other times Ma made me hold my hands up high, and she slipped the dresses over my head. *Then* I felt the soft new cloth brush against my face. (*Forgetting the shoe.*) It was the feel of the cloth against my skin just now, I guess. But, when I slipped my white dress off, it was like—like somethin' slippin' away from me... somethin' I wanted... and couldn't ever have.

JOE (*puzzled*). I reckon fine clothes remind you of the times you had to stand still while Ma pinned patterns on you.

MARTIE (*retouching the shoe*). I never got tired. (*Looking up.*) I stood up straight—and still, like Ma told me.

JOE. Ma and I always said you looked better in them fine clothes than the folks that owned 'em.

MARTIE (*putting the painted shoe on the hearth and going back to the table*). That didn't make it any easier, Joe. I always had to take off the pretty dresses and put on my old ones. I've done it a thousand times, I reckon. (*Painting the other shoe.*) At Sunday-school I sat lookin' at dresses I'd seen myself in, in Ma's bureau mirror. And my own dress was faded and too tight. At school girls pointed at my old dresses pieced out with scraps that matched their clothes, and giggled. Sometimes they just whispered but I knew what they were sayin'. (*Her emotion mounting.*) One girl used to sidle up to me when the *patches* of my old dress matched the new dress she was wearin' (*Her voice almost breaking.*)—so everybody would know Ma had used her scraps!

JOE (*sympathetically*). I didn't know it was *that* bad, Martie.
(*There is a rap on the front door.*)

MARTIE (*as* JOE *starts to rise*). I'll go, Joe! (*She runs toward the door but suddenly remembers her bare feet.*) Hand me my shoes, Joe! (*Snatching up the shoe from the table and slipping it on while* JOE *picks up the shoe on the hearth and brings it to her.*) There's no tellin' *who* it is. (*As she slips on the shoe,* MELISSA *comes into the room. There is another rap and* MELISSA *goes toward the door.* MARTIE *scampers across the floor, opens the door a little way, and steps out on the porch, closing the door behind her.*)

MELISSA. Well, I wonder what she's up to, now.

JOE. Oh, just somebody stoppin' by to talk about the dance, I reckon.

MELISSA (*drawing back the curtain of the window and peering out*). It's the mail-carrier; he's handin' her a letter. (*Turning to* JOE.) I knowed she was up to sumpum.

JOE (*putting the clothes in the basket*). Wonder who could be a-writin' to us? We ain't had nothin' but seed catalogues since them mail boxes was put up in front o' the commissary. Cayn't be nothin' more'n a advertisement for chill-tonic or sumpum though. But sure was nice o' old Bill to come out o' his way and bring it to the house.

MELISSA (*glancing from the window to* JOE *as he sets the basket under the table.*) Cause you ain't had no letters, ain't no reason Martie ain't wrote none.

JOE. Aw, Lissie, who'd Martie be a-writin' to? She sees near 'bout ever'body in Shady Grove ever'time she goes to the commissary. And them she don't see there, she sees at church of a Sunday.

MELISSA (*looking out the window*). The mail-man's gone, now. (*In an excited voice as she pulls the curtain farther back.*) She's a-openin' it! She must be a-readin' it, but her lips ain't movin'. (*She runs to the door and flings it open. Sarcastically, as* MARTIE *comes in, the open letter in her hand.*) Come on in. I cayn't read, you know! (*Looking at* MARTIE *searchingly.*) You don't tell me you heerd fum yo' town feller? You been a-writin' to *him*, I reckon.

MARTIE (*in a strained voice as she comes forward*). Yes, I wrote to him. I was afraid he'd forget about the spring gatherin'. I . . . I invited him *special* . . . to come to this dance.

JOE. Well you sure don't look joyful 'bout his comin'.

MARTIE (*letting the letter and envelope slip from her hands to the floor.*) He's . . . he's not comin', Joe.

MELISSA (*folding her arms*). Whatever put it in yo' head he was comin'? He never come back fer them other dances.

MARTIE. I thought maybe he . . . forgot. So I . . . I reminded him . . . this time. (*To* JOE, *as if appealing for an explanation.*) But he . . . he said he liked the Commissary dance. He said it was more fun than the dances in town. When I told him we wanted him to come again, he said he'd be glad to come. . . . (*Her voice breaking as she sinks down in the rocker.*) And I've been . . . countin' on the spring dance.

MELISSA. Well, why ain't he comin'?

MARTIE. He's too far away . . . he says.

JOE (*crossing back of the rocker and looking down at* MARTIE). Pshaw, what you care? Plenty mo' boys to dance with, tonight. And maybe he'll come next time. Maybe he won't be so far away, then.

MARTIE. No, he won't ever come back. I feel it. (*Looking straight before her as she sits slightly sidewise on her chair.*) That night I was with him was like the times I saw myself all fine in the mirror... in things that didn't belong to me. It was like when Ma took me to Montgomery once and showed me the things in the store windows... things I couldn't have... just look at... I ought to have known it would be like this. I reckon I did halfway know it, when I took my white dress off awhile ago... and felt somethin' slippin' away from me....
(MELISSA *watches* MARTIE *curiously. She stares at her silvered shoes and, after a glance at the pine table, picks up the bottle of silver paint.*)

MELISSA (*contemptuously*). Silver shoes! A nice way fer a po' farmer to spend his money. (*She goes to the fireplace, hurls the bottle to the hearth where it shatters, the silver paint spattering on the floor.*)

MARTIE (*rising as* MELISSA *turns angrily toward her*). Keep your words, Melissa! I'm not puttin' up with any more from you tonight—or any other time!

JOE. Go put on your pretty dress, Martie. I'll walk over to the dance with you.

MARTIE (*hopelessly*). It'll be the same thing when we come back, Joe. It'll always be like this... with me here. I... I reckon I come between you and Lissie.

JOE. You know I always promised Ma I'd give you a home, Martie. And it's nothin' but right.

MARTIE. It's different now, Joe. You ... you're married now, and it's ... different.

MELISSA (*as* MARTIE *turns to the door*). Where you goin' in that ol' dress o' mine and a rose in yo' hair? (*Laughing sarcastically.*) You sure look like ketchin' a town beau, now.

MARTIE (*her hand on the door*). Nancy Bell can have my white dress, Lissie. Let her dress up and *play* lady! She'll never be one—not with you to bring her up! (*Hopelessly to herself.*) And I won't be wearin' party dresses any more.

JOE (*taking a step toward her*). Where you goin', Martie?

MARTIE. Maybe I'll walk over to Hamp's store and tell him to send a bottle of medicine for Joey.

JOE. But yo' shoes ain't dry, Martie. The mud'll ruin 'em.

MARTIE (*grimly*). Hamp Walker's wife won't be needin' silver shoes. (*She goes out softly and the door closes after her.*)

CURTAIN

THE IVORY SHAWL

A PLAY OF THE BACK COUNTRY

Written in the playwriting course at the University of North Carolina and originally produced by The Carolina Playmakers, July 19, 1937.

THE CHARACTERS

HAMP WALKER, *owner of a small cross-roads store in southern Alabama*	Clemon White
MATTIE, *his wife*	Marian Tatum
MARTHA, *his daughter*	Rietta Bailey
LIZE, *his unmarried sister*	Pearl Fishel
SAM BOGAN, *a neighboring young farmer*	James Decker

SCENE: The Walkers' livingroom adjoining a cross-roads store in a remote section of southern Alabama.

TIME: The present. A late afternoon in early February.

THE SCENE

The scene is the livingroom of the Walker farmhouse in a remote section of southern Alabama. It is a late afternoon in February and the low blaze in the crude rock fireplace in the center of the left wall has begun to cast softening shadows over the drab furnishings.

MATTIE WALKER, *a thin faded woman of forty, with graying brown hair drawn close to her head and wound in a knot at the back, is sitting before the hearth in a rockerless, splint-bottomed chair. Now and then she leans forward to stir something she is cooking on the fire. On the floor beside her chair, is a pan of potatoes in an uncovered boiler of water. On the hearth are an iron kettle and a coffee pot. Seated at her right, in a chair drawn farther back from the fire her spinster sister-in-law,* LIZE, *is crocheting.* LIZE, *awkward and sharp-featured, is sour and severe of mien. Both women wear drab calico and coarse shoes and stockings.* MATTIE'S *long-sleeved shirtwaist dress is faded and worn. A dark-blue, checkered apron partially covers her skirt. Her heavy black shoes, a size too large, are run down at the heels.*

In the right corner of the room is an old high-backed wooden bed covered with a "crazy quilt." At the foot of the bed is a small, dilapidated trunk and against the right wall is an old-fashioned walnut bureau with cracked mirror. On the marble top of the bureau is an old-fashioned "dressing-table set" of china.

In the center of the bare floor is an unpainted pine

table covered with a red-figured cotton cloth. On it are large pewter salt- and pepper-shakers, and a heavy glass syrup-pitcher and sugar bowl. A plate, turned down, a cup and saucer, "silver" that was once plated, a napkin in a bone ring, and several wooden serving spoons, are on the table before a splint-bottomed chair. Another chair is pushed close to the left of the table. A golden-oak rocker with arms, the only piece of furniture not in a state of dilapidation, stands at the right of the table. Behind the rocker by the bed, is a quilting-frame on which is stretched an unfinished "log cabin" quilt of vari-colored scraps of calico.

In the center of the rear wall is a door leading to HAMP WALKER'S *small general store. To the right of this door are pegs set in a diamond-shaped wooden frame. On one of the pegs hang* HAMP WALKER'S *sleazy woollen coat and shapeless, wide-brimmed felt hat. To the left of the store door is an old walnut food-safe, a cupboard with wooden doors forming its base, and perforated tin doors covering rows of shelves above. To the left of the foodsafe is a small table supporting a granite wash-bowl and pitcher, and a cedar water-bucket with a gourd dipper. A large pail stands beside the table; hanging on the wall above it are cooking utensils and a dish-pan. At the left are two shelves containing mis-matched crockery, chipped or cracked, and thick drinking glasses. A rollertowel hangs below the shelves.*

Beyond the fireplace is the pantry door and down-left is a door leading to other rooms of the house. On the mantel are an old-fashioned clock in a wooden frame, a kerosene-lamp of glass, and a box of matches. A woodbox filled with logs of hickory and oak partially covered by "light'ood knots" stands against the left wall, between the fireplace and the lower door. At the right of the wood-box is a home-made broom of long grasses. No pictures adorn the rough-boarded, unpainted walls.

LIZE (*looking up from her crocheting*). You're sp'ilin' Marthie, Matt. Why don't you wait and make *her* git supper when she comes?

MATTIE. Martha does her part, Lize—more'n her share.

LIZE (*sourly*). She's goin' to grow up jes' like them four boys o' yourn—no manner of account to nobody.

MATTIE. Lize, you know how Hamp kept the boys out o' school to work the field and help in the store. And anyhow, there ain't no chance for a boy here at the Cross Roads.

LIZE (*her eyes on her crocheting*). Well, we'll see how yo' high-minded Marthie turns out.

MATTIE (*glancing at the clock*). It's about time the graduatin' exercises was over.

LIZE (*looking up at the clock*). She oughter been home 'fore now. Hit's 'most five o'clock. (*Sarcastically, as* MATTIE *stoops to stir the pot over the fire.*) I'd have thought you'd have been there to see yo' pretty Marthie take off first honors.

MATTIE (*sitting back in her chair*). I didn't have nothin' fittin' to wear, (*Glancing down at her shabby shoes and running her hand over her faded dress.*) and I wouldn't want Martha's friends to see me like this. Besides, Hamp's got Cliff and Jim plowin' the horse in the field today and I wa'n't equal to the walk.

LIZE. Well, hit's high time Cliff and Jim finished that plowin'. Here 'tis February, and not a seed in the ground. But I reckon you think *yo'* boys oughter be in school, 'stead o' workin'.

MATTIE (*hopelessly, more to herself than to* LIZE). They'd have learned quick enough if Hamp hadn't stopped 'em. But they ain't like Martha. Tom and Jerry's not like their sister, either. None o' the boys'll ever go back to school, now that Hamp's put 'em to work.

LIZE. Marthie gits her ways after that school-teachin' pa o' yourn. Well, yo' ma never had no easy time fer all his larnin', and her'n, too.

MATTIE. Lize, you know how Pa died when all of us was little, and Ma had to stay home and tend us. That's why she couldn't do no better by me—why I never finished school and all that.

(MARTHA, *a pretty girl of seventeen, neatly dressed in crisp, light-blue gingham, a hand-knitted, navy-blue sweater and small matching hat, hurriedly comes in through the store door at the rear. She is breathless from running, her dark eyes shining with excitement.*)

MARTHA (*proudly*). Well, here it is, folks! (*She unrolls her diploma and holds it up for* MATTIE *and* LIZE *to see. Then, impulsively, she crosses to her mother.*)

You're to have the first look, Ma. (*She stands by* MATTIE's *chair and leans over her, stroking her hair as they silently read it together.*)

MATTIE (*looking up*). You've done well, Martha. But I'm sorry you couldn't have waited and graduated at the big exercises next June 'stead o' finishin' up in the middle o' the year. (MATTIE *hands the diploma to* LIZE *who fingers it curiously.*)

MARTHA (*laughing a little, as she hangs her hat and sweater on pegs by the door*). I'm afraid we couldn't have held out against Pa that long. And I guess February's as good a month as any to graduate in.

LIZE (*handing the diploma back to* MARTHA). Now we'll see what good hit does you.
(MARTHA, *ignoring the remark, takes pins from the china tray on the bureau and attaches the diploma to the wall near her mother's bed.*)

MARTHA (*stepping back to regard the diploma with pride*). It's *yours*, Ma. You worked the hardest for it. Cooking, and washing and ironing—and sewing 'way late at night—slaving here alone so I could have time to study. (*She goes to the food-safe, opens a door of the cupboard, takes out an apron, and slips it on.*) Isn't this the night Pa goes to the lodge meetin', Ma?

MATTIE. Yes, and he'll be a-wantin' early supper. I've got his place set and we'll let him eat first. (*She pokes up the fire and* MARTHA *sets the boiler of peeled potatoes over the blaze. There is a rap on the store door.*

LIZE, *always curious, hurries to answer. She drops her ball of thread and it unwinds behind her as she carries her needles and unfinished work with her. She cracks the door open and peeps out.*)

LIZE (*opening the door a little more and thrusting her head out*). Ev'nin', Sam. Marthie's jes' got home. Come on in and set a spell.
(SAM BOGAN, *a stocky, red-faced youth with stiff, unruly white hair, enters timidly. He is wearing a new suit of reddish brown, a bright green shirt, a brighter tie and socks, and shiny, light-tan shoes. He stands awkwardly, fumbling a cheap blue-gray felt hat in his roughened hands.*)

MATTIE (*rising hurriedly and wiping her hands on her apron*). Howdy, Sam. Sit down, won't you?

SAM (*letting* MATTIE's *hand fall after giving her a clammy hand-shake*). I guess I won't be a-stayin' this time, Mrs. Walker. It's so pretty out, I kinder thought Martha might like to go car-ridin'—if she ain't too busy.

MATTIE. That's nice of you, Sam. (*Turning to* MARTHA.) Martha—

MARTHA. I'm helping Ma, now, Sam. (*Turning back to her cooking.*) Some other time....

MATTIE (*going to the fireplace*). You run along, Martha, I'll have supper ready in no time. 'Bout all I've got to do now is dish it up.

MARTHA (*rising from the hearth*). The corn bread's not cooking fast, Ma. I'd better get you some light-bread from the store. (*Her hand on the door-knob.*) I'll be back in just a minute, Sam. (*To* MATTIE *as she opens the door.*) Get out a jar of your fig preserves, Ma, and maybe Pa won't mind cold bread so much. (*She goes into the store.*)

MATTIE. 'Scuse me a minute, Sam. (SAM *nods and* MATTIE *hurries through the pantry door.*)

LIZE (*winding her trailing thread on the ball*). Set down, Sam, since you got to wait. Law, my legs would a-caved in under me long ago, ifn I'd stood up ever' time I waited on sumpum in this house.
(SAM *pulls out a chair from the table and sits.*)

LIZE (*in the rocker, beginning to disentangle her thread*). I been hearin' a pow'ful lot o' hammerin' down yo' way, Sam. I reckon you 'bout got yo' house all finished, ain't you?

SAM. Yas'm. Them city carpenters works right fast. Jes' 'bout done over the old place.

LIZE. Well, yo' pa sho' fixed you up nice when he died.

SAM. Yas'm. House wa'n't much. But hit's good land.

LIZE (*beginning to crochet*). All that white paint and them new green winder-blinds looks mighty pretty, Sam. Ain't nothin' like that never been seen at the Cross Roads befo'.

SAM. Naw'm, I reckon not. But I figgered a girl like Martha, she ... she'd ...

LIZE. Maybe she kin git some sense in her head, now she's got that diplomie off her mind!
SAM (*nervously twirling his hat*). Yas'm. I figgered she ... she might be willin' to settle down after she'd done gone clear thoo high school. (*Laughing awkwardly.*) 'Tain't nothin' left 'er to do, now, 'cept settle down.
(MATTIE *returns with a jar of fig preserves which she places on the table and* MARTHA *comes back from the store. There is a moment of embarrassment for* SAM. MARTHA *places the bread on the table and begins to untie her apron strings as* SAM *rises.*)

MATTIE. You'd better stay and eat with us, Sam.

SAM. Not tonight, Ma'am. (*Awkwardly to* MARTHA, *as he turns to leave.*) I guess I ... I'll be a-crankin' up, Martha.

MARTHA (*placing her apron in the cupboard*). I'll be right on, Sam.
(SAM *goes out through the store.* MATTIE *returns to her cooking.* MARTHA *takes her hat and sweater from the wall.*)

LIZE (*still crocheting as* MARTHA *goes to the mirror and puts on her hat and sweater*). Well, if he asks you, you'd better take 'im. He's the best ketch 'round here —good as *you'll* ever do.
(MARTHA, *without replying, turns from the bureau and crosses to the store door.*)

MARTHA. I'll be back early to help you, Ma.

MATTIE. Don't you hurry back for me, Martha.

LIZE (*as* MARTHA *smiles back at her mother before leaving*). *Early*, humph! Tain't what I call early now. (*Rising and holding out the unfinished yoke she is crocheting.*) Well, who'd have thought this gown yoke would have tuck up another ball o' thread. Skimpy's what I calls them balls. 'Tain't nothin' good as hit useter be. (*Crossing to store door.*) I'll bet I have a time a-matchin' this thread, the way Hamp and them boys keeps things tumbled up in that store. (*She bustles out, slamming the door behind her.* MATTIE *lifts a boiler from the fire and sets it on the hearth. She rises wearily, her stooped form and the expression on her face depicting utter hopelessness as she drags her ill-fitting shoes across the floor. She takes a plate from the shelf and a bread-knife from the food-safe and carries them to the table where she unwraps the bread and places it on a plate. She takes the wrapping-paper into the pantry and returns with a crock of butter, a small pitcher of milk, cheese, and a glass of buttermilk, which she sets before her husband's plate.*)

MATTIE (*as* MARTHA *returns and hangs up her coat and sweater*). Why didn't you go car-ridin' with Sam, Martha?

MARTHA. I told him to come back for me later, Ma. I ... I wanted to tell you something. Somehow, I ... I couldn't tell you before Aunt Lize.

MATTIE. You mean you've told Sam, final, you'd marry 'im?

MARTHA. No, Ma, I haven't ever said "yes" or "no" to Sam. It's not that. It's... Oh, Ma! (*Bubbling over.*) I... I won the scholarship, Ma!

MATTIE (*in a low voice, dazed*). One o' *mine*... one o' mine's won the scholarship....

MARTHA. Why not, Ma? Why shouldn't one of us win, same as anyone else?

MATTIE. I don't know, Martha. I'd jes' sort o' give up, I reckon. I didn't expect nothin' more for none of us.

MARTHA. It's to the State Normal, Ma. If I make good, I can teach in two years and get a good salary! But it's not that, Ma. It's going on learning things that's so wonderful. (*Wistfully.*) Things folks don't know much about here at the Cross Roads. (*Glancing around the room.*) And it's getting away from here, Ma. (*Placing her arms about her mother.*) Not that I want to leave you, Ma, but— Oh, Ma, do you think Pa'll let me go?

MATTIE (*folding her arms*). When does it start?

MARTHA. The second term begins right away, but I can wait a week or two, if I must. (*Eagerly.*) I'll catch up. (HAMP, *a stout, florid, middle-aged man, comes in from the store. He is coatless, with baggy gray trousers held up by gaudy suspenders. He notes with a scowl that his supper is not ready.*)

HAMP. With three women in the house, it does look like they could git a man's victuals done on time.

MATTIE (*quietly, as she takes the coffee-pot from the hearth and sets it on the embers*). We'll get you to the lodge meetin' on time, Pa.

HAMP (*turning to* MARTHA). Well, what's ailin' *you?*

MARTHA. I . . . I just got in, Pa. We'll have your supper ready in a minute. (*She pokes up the fire.*)

HAMP. Humn, jes' got in, eh? Where you been?

MARTHA (*nervously*). I . . . I finished at the County High today. (*Nodding toward the wall.*) See, there's my diploma hanging by the bed.
(HAMP *walks over to the bed and studies the diploma, grunts and sits down heavily at the table.* MATTIE *takes a dish of left-over snap-beans from the food-safe, empties them in a boiler, pours water over them, and places them on the fire.*)

MATTIE. The corn bread'll be done in a minute, Pa.

MARTHA. Would you like another glass of buttermilk, Pa?
(HAMP *shakes his head in refusal as he serves himself to preserves.* MARTHA *slices bread for him.*)

MARTHA (*glancing toward* MATTIE *now stooping over the hearth*). Can I get you a cup of coffee, Pa? Ma's got it ready now.

HAMP (*cramming bread sopped in preserve syrup*), Oughter been ready when I come in.
(MATTIE *brings the coffee-pot and the smoking boiler of beans from the fire.* MARTHA *pours a cup of coffee for her father while* MATTIE, *at* HAMP's *left, generously serves his plate with beans.* MATTIE *takes both utensils back to the fireplace, sets them on the hearth and covers the beans.*)

MARTHA (*pouring milk in* HAMP's *coffee*). I ... I won the scholarship, Pa.
(HAMP *puts down his fork, leans back in his chair, runs his thumbs under his suspenders and regards his daughter with a look of mingled curiosity and suspicion.*)

HAMP. What the hell's that? You ain't been mixed up in that rafflin' game down at Lige Palmer's commissary, have you?

MARTHA. Of course not, Pa. I made good grades at the County High and that entitled me to the scholarship—two years at the State Normal—tuition free!

HAMP. Well you ain't a-goin'!

MARTHA. Please, Pa.—It won't cost much, with the scholarship. And afterwards I can get a good job and help out at home.

HAMP (*rising*). You'll help out at home now, and from now on. You'll help with the cookin' and sewin', and the washin' and ironin'. Been 'way from home too much, a'ready. That's what's the matter with you, now.

THE IVORY SHAWL 139

But—(*Reaching for a piece of cheese and swallowing it hurriedly.*) if you don't like the home you got, go and git you a husband.
(MATTIE *crosses to her quilting-frame and watches* HAMP *furtively.*)

MARTHA. Oh, Pa, it would only be two years at the Normal.
(HAMP *sets down his coffee and strides over to the fireplace.* MARTHA *follows him, fearful but eager.*)

HAMP. You ain't a-goin', I tell you! I've got no patience with this here high book-larnin' fer women. It puts notions in their heads. (*Pacing the floor.*) If you're so bent on leavin' here, you'll do well to take Sam. I guess he's asked you times enough. Why ain't you had 'im, befo'?

MARTHA. Oh, Pa, Sam's all right, but—

HAMP. But *what?* Ain't he good as any farmer 'roun' here? Ain't he got the best place at the Cross Roads?

MARTHA. But Pa, I worked for the scholarship. I earned it. And I want it!

MATTIE (*looking up from her quilting*). There ain't no hurry 'bout her marryin', Pa. Sam'll wait, I reckon.

HAMP (*glaring at* MATTIE). Then git them notions out o' her head! If ever I see her nose stuck in one o' them books agin, I'll burn the last one of 'em! (*Striding toward the mantle, his hands clenched in a fit of anger.*) Where's that blamed thing, anyhow? (*Snatches the diploma from the wall.*) So that's what the County High done for you—puttin' notions in yo' head 'bout leavin' yo' folks.

MARTHA (*helplessly, as he crushes the diploma*). Oh, Pa....
(HAMP *strides to the fireplace and hurls the diploma on the blazing coals.*)

LIZE (*coming in from the store*). Sam's come back fer you, Martha. I reckon he's anxious to show off his fine house.

HAMP. Git yo' hat, Martha. Sam's been hangin' 'roun' the store 'most all ev'nin'. You've had 'im waitin' on you long enough.

MARTHA (*quietly*). I'm not going.

HAMP (*clutching her by the shoulder and shaking her*). Don't you say that to me, d'ye hear? (*Shaking her again.*) You clear out o' here, and don't you come back till you git rid o' them high-soundin' notions! (*He releases her and she crosses slowly to the store door.*) And you better talk nice to Sam, d'ye hear?

MARTHA (*wearily*). Yes, Pa.... (*Listlessly, she takes her hat and sweater from the wall and leaves.*)

HAMP (*contemptuously, to* LIZE). See if you kin keep store till closin' time. (*He reaches for his hat and coat and goes out, slamming the door behind him.*)

MATTIE (*quietly, as* LIZE *stands folding up her work*).
Tell the boys they can get their supper now.
(LIZE *goes out the door leading to the store and* MATTIE *begins to transfer the dishes from the supper table to the smaller table by the wall. She picks up the iron kettle from the hearth, sets it on the fire, takes the dish-pan from its nail above the table, scrapes the dishes, and piles them in the pan. The store door opens and* MATTIE *looks up as* MARTHA—*a different* MARTHA *with zest in life gone—comes in slowly.*)

MATTIE. Where's Sam, Martha?

MARTHA. I told him I'd see him tomorrow. Pa had rushed off to the lodge meeting with Tom and Jerry.

MATTIE. I hope yo' pa don't find out you didn't go ridin' with Sam, and get in another temper. Better call Jim and Cliff and I'll warm you-all up somethin'.

MARTHA. Jim and Cliff said tell you they were going to bed and wouldn't want any supper. Jerry carried them a lunch from the store while they were plowing the field.

MATTIE (*taking a glass from the shelf and placing it by a clean plate on the table*). They're wore out, I guess. Well, sit down and eat somethin', yourself.

MARTHA. I'm not hungry, Ma. You sit down and I'll do the dishes.

MATTIE. Tom and Jerry's got to eat when they come in from the lodge meetin'. And Lize can't eat till closin' time. (*Going toward the dining table and picking up the preserve jar, pitcher, and crock of butter.*) We'll wait and do all the dishes at once.

MARTHA (*indifferent*). I guess I'll be sewing, then. (*She goes out door at left.*)
(MATTIE *lights the lamp on the mantel and places it on the pine table.* MARTHA *returns with a work-basket and a rose-colored lamp-shade. She places the lamp-shade on the lamp, which casts a soft glow over the room. She sits at left of table and begins to sew on something fluffy and pink.* MATTIE *goes to the food-safe and takes out a pan of peas.*)

MATTIE (*sitting down in the rocker*). 'Pears like it takes so long to shell peas and string beans. If I don't get it done at night, I don't never get to it next day. (MARTHA *measures a pink ribbon over her shoulder and clips it with embroidery scissors.*) Well, I suppose you told Sam, final, after what yo' pa said.

MARTHA. Not yet, Ma. But I've about made up my mind to it.

MATTIE. He'll be a-wantin' you right away, Martha, after waitin' so long. (*After a pause.*) But you've about got everything ready, haven't you?

MARTHA. I got almost everything ready last summer, Ma, before ever I decided to marry Sam. You know how Pa kept giving me cloth from the store, encouraging me to take him. I thought I might as well make the cloth into things while I could get it. But after I heard about the scholarship and got to working for it, somehow marrying just went out of my head.

MATTIE. Well, Martha, Sam'll give you a good comft'able home. You won't ever have to slave and worry to make ends meet. And that's sayin' a whole lot.

MARTHA. Sam showed me the house when I was passing by on the way to school this morning, Ma.

MATTIE. I guess he had it done over for *you*.

MARTHA. He said so, Ma. But I haven't ever said "yes," yet, and he knows it. He's had the house fixed just like he thought I'd like it, though. Two men came down from Montgomery and did it.

MATTIE. Well, Martha, it's sumpum to see you start out right. When yo' pa and me was first married, he said he'd build a better house some day, and he let me lay up the money from eggs and butter I sold. (*Wistfully*.) I kept that up a long time, thinkin' I'd buy pretty things for the new house. (*Wearily*.) But yo' pa jes' kept a-tackin' shed rooms onto the store as we needed 'em, and I jes' give up after 'while.

MARTHA. Have you seen Sam's house from the road, Ma?

MATTIE (*shaking her head*). I ain't had time to walk down there.

MARTHA (*placing her sewing on the table, enthusiastic for the first time*). It's a *painted* house. And oh, Ma, the kitchen's going to have a nice floor and curtains!

And Ma, the parlor's got wall-paper, with pink roses running all over it. Sam put most of the old furniture in the barn. He said he thought I might like to choose the new furniture, myself. Said he'd take me to Montgomery to get it as soon as we were married.

MATTIE. You make him go 'forehand, Martha. Sam's a good honest boy, but— You do what I say.

MARTHA. There's just one thing about that house, Ma. (MATTIE *looks up inquiringly*.) I've never seen a book or a picture on the place, Ma. And now Sam's built shelves for dishes and shelves for bedding, and everything a person could use shelves for—except books. We'll get some books when we go to Montgomery for furniture, of course; but it seems so *funny* —money, and a fine house, and nothing to read. It got me to thinking how ... how different we are ... Sam and I.

MATTIE. Nothin's goin' to interest Sam but the farm, Martha. He's like yo' pa in some ways.

MARTHA (*puckering her brow over a needle hard to thread*). I guess I oughtn't to expect too much of Sam, his folks being like they were and his pa letting him quit school in the fourth grade—But it just came over me, Ma, after seeing the house, that ... that Sam and I wouldn't ever do things together—*you* know—like reading, and all that.

MATTIE (*practically*). Sam's not had much schoolin', Martha, and he's not much to look at. But I can rest easy you'll be taken care of.

(MARTHA *folds the lingerie and goes over to the trunk at the foot of the bed. Lifting the top of the trunk, she lays the lingerie inside.*)

MARTHA (*kneeling beside the trunk*). It's 'most full, Ma. Would you like to take a peep? (MATTIE *places the pan of peas on the table and goes over to the trunk.*)

MATTIE. They look real pretty, Martha—folded nice and neat, too, jes' like you was all packed to go.

MARTHA. But this is your trunk, Ma—the only place you have to keep your things.

MATTIE (*stroking* MARTHA's *hair*). I'll find somewhere else to put 'em, Martha. You can have the trunk to move in. I don't never expect to go trav'lin', nohow.

MARTHA. Haven't you ever been away from the Cross Roads, Ma?

MATTIE. Not since I married. Seemed like I never could catch up with the work to get away. And we never had the money to spare for trips after Lize come to live with us. (*Walking away and pausing with a backward glance at the trunk.*) There ain't much there, and they ain't so fine, Martha; but they're made o' the best yo' pa carries in the store—ever' bit as good as any girl 'round here ever had.

MARTHA (*taking out of the trunk a yellowed, silk hand-painted box tied with a faded, lavender ribbon*). May I open this box now, Ma?—You know you always said I could have it when I grew up.

MATTIE. That box ain't been opened since I was a girl, Martha. But, now you're gettin' married, I reckon you might as well have it.

MARTHA. I've wondered what was in it ever since I was a little girl, Ma. May I really open it now?

MATTIE (*seating herself in the rocker and taking up the pan of peas*). If you wanter.
(MARTHA *unties the ribbon, unwinds it, raises the cover and draws out a large, hand-embroidered shawl of ivory silk. With a sharp breath, she utters a little exclamation of delight.*)

MARTHA (*unfolding the shawl and feeling the thick satiny fringe*). Oh, Ma, isn't it beautiful! It's silk, too! I never knew you had anything fine like this. (*She drapes the shawl around her mother who looks at it without touching it.*)

MATTIE. You put it on, Martha. (*Glancing down at her hands.*) It don't become these old red knotted hands o' mine. *You* wear it. . . .

MARTHA. It . . . it's all you've got in this world that's pretty, Ma. . . .

MATTIE. I don't have no need for it, Martha. (*Pressing the shawl into* MARTHA'*s hands.*) And anyhow, my rough ol' hands'd pick up the silk threads and ruin it. (*To herself, without resentment.*) Fine things don't become me no more.

THE IVORY SHAWL 147

MARTHA (*caressing the shawl*). I never knew you had anything lovely like this, Ma.—I'm glad, Ma; I'm glad you...had...nice...things, once....

MATTIE. That was my mother's shawl, Martha.

MARTHA (*examining the embroidery on the shawl*). And did you wear it when you grew up, Ma? (*She walks to the mirror and drapes the shawl becomingly over her shoulders, primps her hair, and turns to her mother.*) Did you wear it out to parties sometimes, Ma?

MATTIE (*without looking up*). Before I was married....

MARTHA. Here's a pressed rose too, Ma. Did you have roses the last time you wore it?

MATTIE (*with suppressed emotion*). Martha...Martha ...Come here....Come here, Martha! Come to the light....Come closer.... (*The rose falls from* MARTHA's *hand.*)

MARTHA. What is it, Ma?

MATTIE. You look like my mother, Martha! I saw her one night a-wearin that shawl. (*She goes to* MARTHA *and lightly touches her daughter's hair.*) Yes, you got hair like hers. You got her eyes and fine white skin. (*Running her hands over* MARTHA's *arms and hands.*) You ain't a Walker, Martha. I always felt it. You're like my mother and her people. I see it, now. (*Touching* MARTHA's *cheek lightly.*) Martha, you're too good for Sam Bogan. You're too good, d'ye hear? He can't have you! The Cross Roads can't have you! (MARTHA *stands silent with wide eyes.*) D'ye hear what I say, Martha? (*Grasping her by the shoulder.*) You've got to get away from the Cross Roads! You can't throw away yo' life like this!

MARTHA. I've never had any place to go outside the Cross Roads, Ma.
(MATTIE *backs away and drops weakly into the chair.*)

MATTIE. Martha, I thought the soul in me had died, drudgin' here year after year and doin' the same things day after day, never hardly raisin' my eyes from my work, never seein' nothin' to lift me up. I've had the spirit crushed out o' me. I been asleep to think o' lettin' you waste yo' life here at the Cross Roads with a man like Sam Bogan.

MARTHA (*fingering the fringe of the shawl*). Pa'll never hear of letting me go to the State Normal, Ma. I'm not so bent on marrying Sam, but—it might as well be that as ... this....

MATTIE (*straightening up*). You sit down there, Martha. You don't know what you're sayin'. You don't know what marryin' means, and it lastin' year in and year out. (*Bringing her clenched hand down on the table.*) Sit down, I tell you! (MARTHA *sits in the straight chair opposite* MATTIE.)

MATTIE. I'm goin' to tell you somethin', Martha—somethin' that's come back to me, seein' you wear that shawl. (*After a pause.*) When my mother died, my brother took me to his house. His wife never wanted me there. I grew up slavin' for that family—and she begrudgin' ever' mouthful I ate, and keepin' me out o' school to nurse and cook.

MARTHA (*softly*). Oh, Ma, and you never had any fun, not even when you were young?

MATTIE. I went out in the ev'nin's some when I begun to grow up. There was parties in the neighborhood now and then. And there was the spring festival with the big square-dance in the commissary ever' year. (*With pride.*) No girl could beat me a-dancin'. (*After a pause.*) I met a boy at the big spring dance one night —a boy that talked different from the rest o' the boys I knew. (*Looking straight ahead of her.*) Walkin' home with me after the festival, he told me about the places he'd been. I was a-wearin' that silk shawl. (*Glancing at the rose on the floor.*) And that rose was in my hair. It all comes back to me now.... I kept hopin' he'd come back. (*Speaking louder and faster.*) But he was jes' passin' through the night I met 'im.... I went to ever' dance after that, hopin' I'd see 'im again. He'd made me b'lieve I was somebody. (*Looking at* MARTHA.)—like I can b'lieve in you, now. But I was just a country girl—somethin' different to the town boy that said square-dancin' was more fun than his town dances. (*After a silence, she looks away.*) After a while, I knew he'd forgot me. And all the time Hamp was a-pressin' me to marry 'im, and my brother and his wife was aggin' it on, thinkin' Hamp was a good catch—like I was thinkin' Sam Bogan was a good catch for you.—But it don't pay, Martha. It

don't pay—this marryin' to get away from somethin'!
It's worse'n what you leave behind, most o' the time.
And a woman had better learn to stand on her own
feet!

MARTHA. But what could you have done, Ma? They
hadn't let you go to school.

MATTIE. I ought to have struck out, anyhow—if I'd
starved tryin' to find work. Anything's better'n sellin'
yo'self! I been a-dyin' inside, here, all these years. I
'most forgot there was pretty things in the world, and
people hopin' and plannin' for better things—like I
heard about the night that boy walked home with me,
and I was a-wearin' that silk shawl. Look at me, now!
Would you think I was ever good to look at? Would
you think I ever wore a thing like that? (*Pointing to
the shawl.*) But it ain't the work that done it. (*Her
breath coming unevenly.*) It's losin' hope o' better
things, when I was young. It's never havin' anybody
to do things with, and see things with, and tell yo' best
thoughts to—jes' shuttin' 'em all up inside o' you,
'cause nobody 'round you would understand... till
after 'while they quit comin'... and somethin' inside
o' you dies....

MARTHA (*leaning forward*). Oh, Ma, you mean—you
think, if I give up Sam, I'll have somebody like that—
somebody to talk to... and... understand?

MATTIE. You might, Martha. You got a better chance
than I had. But, whether you do, or whether you don't,
hold on. Hold on to the best that's in you.

MARTHA. Oh, Ma, how'd we ever tell all that to Pa, and he so bent on my marrying Sam?

MATTIE. Tell 'im nothin'! Jes' clear out 'fore he comes back.—Go tell Cliff I said hitch up that horse.

MARTHA. But Cliff's asleep, Ma.

MATTIE. You do what I say. You're goin' to town and take that train for the State Normal *tonight!*

MARTHA. Oh, Ma...! (*She starts toward the door but stops and turns.*) But the ticket, Ma? Where's the money coming from for the ticket—and the books and things?

MATTIE (*resolved*). You do what I say.
(*As* MARTHA *goes out,* MATTIE *takes a knife from the food-safe, goes to the trunk, rips the lining of the top, and draws out a fold of bills.*)

MATTIE (*looking up as* MARTHA *returns*). This is the savin's from the butter and eggs I sold. It'll give you a start. And you'll find a way to get along, once you get there.

MARTHA. I can't take your money, Ma. Keep it. And buy you something nice to wear.

MATTIE (*sharply*). Take it! (*Forcing the money into* MARTHA's *hands.*) Take it, I tell you! (MATTIE *takes the tablecloth from the table, hurries to the trunk, and rolls up an armful of* MARTHA's *clothes.* MARTHA *goes to her room returning presently with a comb, brush, other toilet articles and a small purse in which she places the bills.)*

MATTIE. The rest o' yo' things'll be sent on as soon as I can find a way to get 'em to you. Now hurry up before yo' pa comes.
(MARTHA *hastily puts on her hat and sweater.* MATTIE *takes the shawl to her.)*

MATTIE. And I guess this shawl of mine might as well be a graduatin' present as a weddin' present. Take it. And wear it, Martha . . . for me. . . . (MARTHA, *without taking the shawl, catches her mother in a silent embrace.)*

MARTHA. I . . . I couldn't, Ma. . . . You—you keep it. . . .
(She takes up the bundle of clothing and, without a backward glance, hurries away. MATTIE, *the shawl in her hand, stands motionless as her eyes follow* MARTHA *out. After a moment, she closes the door softly and sinks wearily into* MARTHA's *chair. Her head bows between her arms outstretched on the table and she buries her face in the folds of the shawl, her hands touching it tenderly. The fringed ivory silk falls over her skirt, contrasting strangely with her worn dress and the sordid room.)*

CURTAIN

www.ingramcontent.com/pod-product-compliance
Lightning Source LLC
Chambersburg PA
CBHW030113010526
44116CB00005B/225